*Combining inspirational colour photographs with practical advice,
The Pleasures of Home series shows you how to decorate your home
in creative ways which reflect your own personality. Each chapter
deals with a particular room, decorated in a specific cultural or
historical style. While a different aspect of home decoration is covered
in each volume, the themes of the chapters are consistent across the
series, so that the books can be used together if desired. Whether you
would like guidelines on how to adapt the main features of each style
or step-by-step instructions and illustrations for particular projects,
you'll find all you need to know in The Pleasures of Home.*

THE PLEASURES OF HOME

PAINT & PAPER

THE PLEASURES OF HOME
PAINT & PAPER
HARRY LEVINSON

CASSELL

First edition 1998 by
Cassell
Wellington House
125 Strand
London WC2R 0BB

Distributed in the United States
by Sterling Co., Inc.
387 Park Avenue South
New York, NY 10016-8810

British Library Cataloguing-in-Publication-Data
A catalogue record of this book is available from the British Library

ISBN 0-304-34628-4 (hardback)
ISBN 0-304-35090-7 (paperback)

Designed by Blackjacks Limited
Illustrated by Kate Simunek
Picture research by Julia Pashley

Printed and bound in Spain

Contents

Introduction

*T*here's no better way to instantly transform a room than with paint or paper. Today a wider selection of paints and wallpapers is available than ever before, while more and more decorative paint effects are being achieved by amateurs. Both paint and paper offer endless possibilities to transform a whole room, enhance architectural features or create stunning and unusual effects.

Perhaps the best-known type of decorative painting is trompe l'oeil, *a French term meaning "to deceive the eye".* Trompe l'oeil *techniques are used to fool anyone who is looking at the work into seeing what the painter wants them to see.*

There are two main ways of doing this. The first is to simulate a surface or material such as marble, stone or wood, as in the projects on Egyptian green marble, bird's eye maple, tortoiseshell and verdigris effects. The second type of trompe l'oeil *involves imitating the three-dimensional world around us. A balustrade, for example, can be painted on a wall, or a ceiling can be painted to look like the sky, as in the sky ceiling project in this book. Alternatively, real textures, surfaces and finishes can be used as a stimulus to create fantasy marble, wood or precious stones.*

The skills and techniques used in replicating luxurious materials in this way have been developed over many centuries. In fact, 3000 years ago, in Ancient Egypt, grainers skilled in replicating rare woods were a professional class of artisans. These skills were also highly valued in Roman times and there still remain many excellent examples of imitation marbles in frescos and trompe l'oeil *mouldings on the walls of Roman buildings.*

In the Victorian era the most famous marbler and grainer was Thomas Kershaw, whose panels were of such beauty and realism that even when you touched them you might still think they were actual marbles and woods. A French newspaper insisted that Kershaw had not painted the samples at all, but had developed some mysterious new method to transfer surfaces from natural marbles and woods.

Today, sadly, skills such as Kershaw's have become rare. However, with the enormous revival of interest in paint effects, and in the use of paper for dramatic effects in decoration, the level of skill is rapidly rising. It would be nice to think that a painter or decorator could enjoy the satisfaction of acquiring some of the skills of a fine artist, and that a fine artist could find gainful employment in producing practical work for interiors using decorative paint techniques. Perhaps the projects in this book, based on such a long tradition of art and craft, will help to preserve these ancient skills.

Materials & Tools

Paints

Paints basically consist of pigment (concentrated colour) mixed with a medium (a form of glue that binds the paint, and dries on contact with air) and a thinner (the oil, water or spirit that makes it workable). Ready-mixed proprietary paint comes in a vast range of colours and a variety of finishes.

Emulsion (latex) is the best-known water-based paint. It can be used on its own or as a basecoat for an oil or water glaze (see below). Emulsion comes in a range of finishes, from matt (flat) through satin/mid-sheen vinyl silk (latex velvet) to gloss. If desired, it can be thinned with water or with emulsion (latex) glaze.

Ready-mixed oil paints include the familiar gloss and eggshell paints. These can be thinned with white spirit (mineral spirits). Eggshell makes a good, hard-wearing undercoat for a glaze.

Distemper (calcimine) was the main type of paint used on walls and ceilings until the middle of this century, when emulsion was introduced. Distemper's flat, dry, chalky quality, rather like old stone, is unsurpassed, and it is now available once more, though not widely. There are various types: whitewash (white or tinted) and oil-based distemper are both easy to use and can be thinned with glaze, but limewash is much trickier. Distemper should be completely removed, or at least treated with a proprietary stabilizer, before being painted over. Otherwise, its powdery texture will prevent the paint from adhering to it.

Artist's colours can be used to tint ready-mixed paints. Emulsion, which is water-based, can be tinted with **artist's acrylics** or **gouache**, both of which are water-based paints that come in tubes. Pigment, mixed with water, can also be used, as can other water-soluble substances such as poster paint, ink or food dye.

For tinting oil paints, **artist's oil colours** may be used, or pigments ground in oil or turpentine.

Chemical dyes known as **universal stainers** (tinting colors) can be used to tint both water-based and oil-based paints. They come in a limited range of intense colours and need to be carefully mixed.

Powder colours are finely ground powders that can be used to tint ready-mixed paints, glazes and varnishes and to make your own glazes and washes. Some are toxic, so follow the precautions on pages 12-13.

Artist's colours may also obviously be used on their own straight from the tube or diluted.

Glazes

Most decorative paint finishes involve working a textured effect into a translucent glaze painted over a base coat which shows through the glaze. A clear glaze, also known as **scumble glaze** or **glazing liquid**, is either oil- or water-based. It can be coloured with artist's colours (oil- or water-based to match the glaze) and thinned as required with white spirit for oil or with water for a water-based glaze. The consistency you'll need will depend on the technique, but the proportions are usually about one part thinner to six or seven parts glaze. Oil glaze can be applied over either an oil-based or a water-based undercoat. A water-based glaze is best applied only over a water-based undercoat. However, it will adhere to an eggshell undercoat if a smooth finish is required. You will need approximately one litre (one US quart) for a

project, depending upon the absorbency of the surface and how thickly you apply it.

Varnishes

The traditional purpose of varnish is to provide a hard protective coating over the decorated surface. It also helps even out the sheen on the surface.

Polyurethane varnish is excellent, as it is strong and coats rapidly to a decent thickness. It comes in matt (flat), semi-matt (eggshell) or gloss finish. **Yacht varnish** provides a very hard-wearing finish that is good for floors.

Oil-based varnishes are also available; though slow-drying, they do give a good finish. **Acrylic varnish**, which is water-based, is quick-drying and does not yellow (unlike oil-based and polyurethane varnishes).

Acrylic-based varnishes, which can be thinned with water, are used over water-based paints/glazes. Polyurethane and oil-based varnishes, which can be thinned with white spirit or turpentine, can be used over either water- or oil-based paints/glazes.

Shellac, which can be thinned with methylated spirit (denatured alcohol), is a spirit-based varnish. It is good for sealing plaster and unpainted wood. The advantage of spirit-based media is that they dry very fast. On the other hand, they are difficult to brush smoothly. Also, this material is reversible; once it has dried hard, it can be dissolved again in methylated spirits – unlike oil – and water-based materials which cannot be redissolved in white spirit or water once they have hardened. Spirit-based varnishes are therefore not very strong and are easily damaged. They do, however, give a wonderful finish when applied competently; in Victorian times they were used to imitate Oriental lacquer.

Applying varnish

To apply varnish, brush it on in first one direction then at right angles using lighter brush strokes, then in the original direction. Allow to dry then apply a second coat.

When this coat is also dry, dampen the surface with water and a little soap. Using dampened very fine wet-and-dry (silicon carbide) paper, rub down the varnish until it feels perfectly smooth.

If a slurry forms on the surface as you work, wipe it away, check for smoothness and continue as necessary. Rinse the wet-and-dry paper in fresh water to clean it.

Once there is no feeling of grit on the surface, you are ready to apply a third coat of varnish. When this is dry, it should be sanded smooth with wet-and-dry once more. Finally, for a perfect finish, rub in a good-quality furniture wax, for a smooth, waxy surface.

Hint
To prevent specks of dust settling on the varnish, sprinkle ( ) spray a little water around your work area.

Oil vs water

Water-based paints can be used for many of the simple, washed effects that are so popular now. Quick and easy to use, they speed up the painting process enormously, and the speed of drying can be increased even more by blowing the surface with a hair dryer.

Oil-based paints are used less today because of concerns about solvents. Another disadvantage is the yellow discoloration that can occur during the drying process. A light blue oil glaze, can become greenish as it dries, and a light pink oil glaze can appear orange. (In fact, a small amount of white eggshell paint can be added to the glaze to prevent this.) However, the slower drying time of oil glazes allows more time to work on it than do water-based glazes, which is valuable for some of the more elaborate finishes. The slower drying time also allows brush marks to settle out, leaving the finished surface smooth and with no trace of brushing.

Great efforts are being made to improve water-based glazes and varnishes as their oil-based equivalents come under increasing pressure from government legislation aimed at eradicating some of the toxins involved. Although the water-based products are becoming more competitive in terms of the results they can achieve, some effects such as top-class marbling still have a better final finish if an oil-based medium is used.

Safety precautions

- Many pigments, varnishes and solvents are toxic, so take great care when using them, protecting your eyes, lungs and skin. Store all materials out of reach of children, and always work in a well-ventilated area.
- Be careful about ventilation when using spray paints, limewash or solvents. Always wear a respiratory mask to protect against inhalation of dangerous fumes.

- Wear chemical-resistant gloves when handling powder colours or limewash. When using powder colours, wear goggles and a paper dust mask as well, to prevent you from inhaling any powder or getting it in your eyes.
- Never smoke, eat or drink when working.
- Solvents are highly flammable. As well as never smoking while working, be careful not to leave paint- or solvent-soaked rags in a pile or in a sealed plastic bag; they could spontaneously combust.
- Goggles are also useful when painting ceilings and sanding surfaces, and dust masks when sanding.

Brushes

Glazes are applied with a variety of implements, such as sponges, brushes, rags or foam rollers. Many of the decorative paint effects included in this book require specialist brushes.

Decorator's brushes are the standard household brushes you can use to apply glaze and eggshell paint. Use a 10cm (4in) brush for large areas, a 2.5cm (1in) brush for small areas and a 5–7.5cm (2–3in) brush for in between.

Sash brushes are small decorator's brushes used for woodwork, and the domed sash has a dome-shaped head. It is useful for pouncing in glaze for marbled and cloud effects.

Varnishing brushes look like decorator's brushes but the bristles are more tightly packed. They give a good finish on varnish but are not used for paint.

Softeners (blenders) are used to blend the edges of paint and obliterate brush marks. The **badger-hair softener** (blender) is the best (and most expensive). For softening thin oil glazes, a **hog's hair softener** is adequate and is cheaper than the badger. For thickly applied oil glazes, start with hog's hair and finish with badger or with a **hakke brush**; the hakke is a Japanese watercolour brush available from art stores, and is much cheaper than badger. For water glazes, only a badger softener will work.

Dusting brushes can be used for stippling small areas that are awkward to get at, for dragging and for the rough softening of glazes on large walls areas being given wash effects.

Fitch brushes are stiff artist's brushes available in different shapes including round or square-ended, and long or short. They are used for small or detailed work.

Pointed, lining or artist's brushes are used for veining, lining and other finely detailed work.

Flogging brushes are long-bristled brushes used for dragging and flogging.

Overgrainers are used for wood-graining. The bristles are grouped into a number of tiny brushes on the larger brush.

Stippling brushes, which come in a variety of sizes and have stiff bristles, are used for lifting off flecks of glaze to give an evenly broken-up surface.

Stencilling brushes are short and round, with stiff, stubby, tightly packed bristles. Pieces of sponge can be substituted for these in many stencilling projects.

Preparation and cleaning

Before beginning to paint, make sure your surface is clean and smooth, without flaking plaster or paint. Any varnish should be sanded down. Fill any holes or cracks with proprietary filler (spackle). If plaster or wood has not been previously painted, prime it with a water-, oil- or spirit-based primer. (Oil- or water-based paints can be used over water-based primer, but water-based paints cannot be used over oil-based primer.) Some primers are toxic, so read the instructions for use carefully, and follow the precautions on page 12.

To clean brushes, remove water-based paints or varnish with warm (not hot) water and soap then rinse and allow to dry. Remove oil-based paints or varnish with white spirit, rinse in soapy water and dry.

> ### Hint
> *If you stop working for an hour or two, prevent your brushes from drying out by covering them with a rag dampened with water (for water-based paints) or turpentine (for oil-based paints). Or simply wrap them in clingfilm (plastic wrap).*

The Country House Style Living Room

THE LIVING ROOM is the heart of the country house.
Here is where you'll find the characteristically
eclectic mix of furniture and knick-knacks – mostly
of high quality but some decidedly eccentric. With their
mellow colours, faded textiles and elegant antiques,
country house living rooms are simultaneously
comfortable and impressive.

Traditionally, country houses have had their walls
decorated with textiles or fine wood panelling, or with
wallpaper or paint effects imitating these. However, a
colourwash can look perfectly suitable in this setting, as
can be seen in the picture on the right. Here, the rough
texture that normally produces a rustic effect gives the
room a look of venerable age. To achieve this effect, a
browny-beige colourwash is applied in the
conventional way (see pages 84-5) but then roughened
slightly by stippling with a coarse brush. Even the
ceiling has been decorated in this way.

The walls of the room on page 16 also have an
interesting textural effect, and the warm colour lends a

*PRECEDING SPREAD:
Create a warm,
cosy look by
colourwashing
walls and ceiling
then adding
texture through
stippling.*

*RIGHT: A simple
stencilled border
and randomly
stencilled stars add
definition to these
colourwashed
walls.*

richness to the room. The technique is the same as that used on pages 38-40, then, in lieu of a cornice, the top edge is finished with a black stencilled border resembling a banner. A few small stars stencilled in gold at random around the walls add a quirky touch.

Texture is created in a different way on the panelled walls of the room on the right. Here the technique involves a form of antiquing – rubbing the top coat of paint back to allow the underneath layer to show through, as in the panelling on pages 121-3. A crackle medium (a medium that reacts with paint to produce the effect of lines of crazing, as you get with old finishes) painted on the surface will add to the effect. Antiquing and crackle medium have also been used for the chair and wainscoting in the picture on page 20.

A similar technique has been used in the room on page 18 (top). In this case, however, bare walls, rather than panelling, have been painted red over white, and then antiqued by rubbing through to the white layer.

An elegant effect can be achieved through the delicate use of glazes, as in the room on page 19. The wall is first painted a pale greenish blue and then glaze in a slightly darker tone is painted on the small infill panels of the bookcase. Bands of the darker glaze are also painted on the walls and on the mouldings to create

straight lines (see page 112). Note the use of shading and *trompe l'oeil* to create three-dimensional effects.

Paint effects in related tones work well on furniture too, creating a traditional look that fits in well with the country house style, however eclectic. On page 18 (bottom) a table has been painted in tones of brown, beige and antique white. Here too the bands can be given a crisp edge using masking tape while painting (see page 112). The simple motif on the front is stencilled on using a tone only a little deeper than the background to give a soft, faded look. To add a feeling of age, you can make up a golden brown glaze and touch in a bit of it where you would expect the table to be slightly darker from years of use.

For a very different effect, cover an old piece of junk furniture with interesting graphic paper. Glue on wallpaper or photocopies of sheet music, antique or

ABOVE: Antiquing will give a look of venerable age to panelling or furniture, and you can emphasize the effect by using crackle medium.

LEFT: Done carefully, sheet music découpaged onto a chest of drawers looks whimsical and chic.

TOP: To achieve a dramatic effect like this, the walls are painted in white emulsion (latex) and colourwashed with a red glaze. The red is then rubbed back to allow the white to show through in places.

BOTTOM: Bands of colour can look sophisticated when toning colours are used.

modern maps, crossword puzzles or some other graphic image. Try enlarging them over and over again on the copier for an even more striking effect. Protect it with varnish, possibly adding a little Burnt Umber for an antique look; or seal the surface with dilute PVA then colourwash, tint or glaze it. This technique is a modern version of découpage in which pictures were cut out and stuck onto a surface, then given about 20 coats of varnish, rubbed down between coats, to make them look like hand painting. Many a country house has boasted attractive pieces of découpage over the centuries, and the idea shown on page 17 (left) is a modern, witty version. It may not be traditional, but one of the attractions of country house style is that there is always a place for eccentric items!

Delicate glazes in tones of greenish-blue add interest to the walls, bookcase and door of this drawing room.

*Antiquing
techniques work
equally well on
wood panelling
and on furniture,
and the effect can
vary from rustic to
elegant.*

Lapis Lazuli Lamp Base

An old, beat-up lamp base can be transformed into a handsome piece using the lapis technique. Boxes and picture frames could also be given the lapis treatment.

Once called "the heaven stone" lapis lazuli is a very beautiful and very expensive stone. The fact that it is found only in some of the world's remotest regions goes some way towards explaining why it has always commanded such a high price. Climbing up into the mountains of Afghanistan or Chile, for example, braving hostile conditions in order to find the caves from which the stones containing the lapis can be mined, has always been a difficult job. Transporting it down out of the mountains to sell to the traders on the coast for export has also been fraught with danger.

During the Renaissance period lapis lazuli was ground into a powder for the brilliant ultramarine blue colour it produced. The powder was so expensive that when a painting was commissioned, the price of the lapis was listed separately.

1 Use a can of gold spray paint to completely cover the lamp base with one coat of gold. Shake the can before starting, to ensure that the paint is thoroughly mixed. Keep the can two or three inches away from the item being sprayed, and move it up and down in a smooth and regular motion until the whole area is evenly coated. Once you have finished, turn the can upside down and continue spraying until the jet stops, otherwise the small hole in the nozzle for the jet will become clogged.

2 Once the gold has dried, apply a very thin coating of oil glaze to the surface of the lamp base.

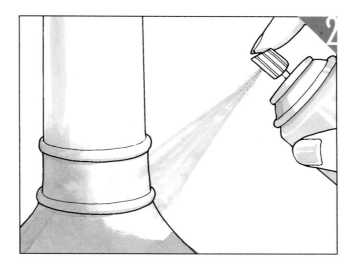

3 The first colour you will apply is Ultramarine, a modern version of the lapis lazuli pigment. Mash a tiny drop of oil glaze into it then, using a fitch brush, tap the Ultramarine onto the lamp in diagonal bands like a loose spiral, leaving irregular spaces rather like lagoons.

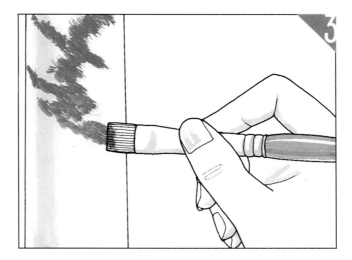

Materials Checklist
- ❁ *7.5cm (3in) decorator's brush*
- ❁ *1.2cm (^{1}/2in) fitch brush*
- ❁ *5cm (2in) hakke brush or badger softener*
- ❁ *Goose feather*
- ❁ *Gold spray paint*
- ❁ *Oil glaze*
- ❁ *Oil paints in Ultramarine and Cerulean Blue*
- ❁ *Bronze powder*
- ❁ *Satin polyurethane varnish*

4 Now tap the second colour, Cerulean Blue, into the lagoons using a second fitch brush.

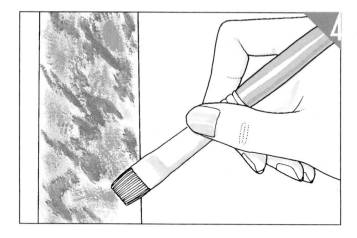

5 Again using a fitch, blend the two colours by softly stippling the whole area. Then, with a Japanese watercolour brush called a hakke, or a badger softener, soften the effect with smooth and gentle brush strokes. (The badger softener is conventionally used for this, but the hakke is a satisfactory and cheaper substitute.) The brush will pick up a heavy coating of these sticky blues, so wipe it often with clean kitchen paper (paper towels).

6 If you look at a necklace of lapis you will see flecks of dark and light blue. You may also see what look like specks of gold in it. To achieve a similar effect, put a little finely ground bronze powder on the edge of a feather and flick it at the lamp. With a little practice, you should be able to flick specks of gold powder into the blue where it will settle and look like the gold in lapis.

7 Gold veins in lapis are seldom evident in the small stones used in jewellery. They can, however, be seen in columns, such as the famous lapis lazuli columns in the Winter Palace at St Petersburg. To imitate the gold veins in the lapis, you need a quill. The quill is the ideal implement for this job; the effect is almost impossible to achieve with a brush. To convert the feather into a quill simply slice off the base of the feather at an angle. Using the pointed edge, gently scrape into the blue to expose a threadlike vein of the base gold.

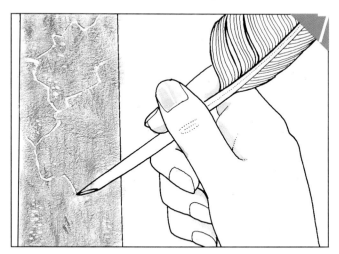

8 Once the lapis effects applied to the lamp have dried thoroughly, varnish with a satin polyurethane varnish as described on page 12.

Hint

When working with bronze powder, it is a good idea to wear a mask, not only to protect your lungs but also to prevent yourself from accidentally blowing on the powder.

Tortoiseshell Jardinière

Using the tortoiseshell technique, inexpensive items can be transformed into beautiful and elegant pieces. Here, a ceramic jardinière has been tortoiseshelled, creating an ideal background for displaying flowers. Surprisingly, the glaze seems to sit on and bind well with the very smooth surface.

Real tortoiseshell came from the shell of the hawksbill turtle. Cut into thin veneers, it was stuck onto, say, the base of a lamp, the back of a comb or a mirror frame. The use of the turtle shell in such a way is now banned.

Genuine tortoiseshell is translucent. The colour comes partly from the material which is placed behind the tortoiseshell veneer. Our project simulates a tortoiseshell which was produced by placing a silvery paper behind the veneer, and which was popular in the Victorian era.

The tortoiseshell is covered with little open spaces of yellow, rather like yellow lagoons. The other colours are dotted all over the surface, like bunches of brown grapes merging into one another. With the technique explained here, you can simulate on a small scale the tortoiseshell that was often used on boxes, mirror frames and the backs of brushes. It is also possible to carry the technique further as a fantasy effect, covering the walls and ceiling of a small room.

Materials Checklist
- ❁ 7.5cm (3in) decorator's brush
- ❁ 1.2cm (1/2in) fitch brush
- ❁ 7.5cm (3in) hog's hair softener
- ❁ 5cm (2in) hakke brush or badger softener
- ❁ Oil paints in Raw Sienna, Raw Umber and Burnt Umber
- ❁ Oil glaze
- ❁ Polyurethane varnish

1 Make up a glaze from Raw Sienna and the same amount of Yellow Ochre mixed with only a small amount of glaze. Daub this yellow-coloured glaze onto the surface to be tortoiseshelled until it is coated evenly.

2 Using the tip of a fitch brush, tap little random clusters of Burnt Umber onto the glaze, as shown below. To soften the edges of the clusters, use a hog's hair softener, giving just one gentle softening stroke.

3 Continue adding more clusters of dots in the same way. As they soften, they will begin to merge into one another all over the area being tortoiseshelled. Slowly you will begin to see little yellow lagoons appearing. When you spot one of these emerging, tap some of the dots around its side to complete the edge, then soften once again, brushing in one direction, with the hog's hair softener.

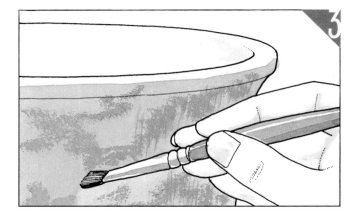

4 Carefully continue with this all over the area until you have a series of little yellow lagoons with clusters of Burnt Umber softened around them. You must be courageous during this stage and carry on adding these little brown dots. If you consciously try to design the yellow spaces beforehand, they end up looking contrived.

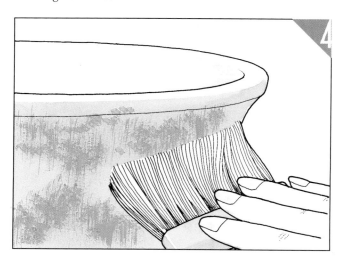

5 Using the tip of a fitch brush, apply some Raw Umber, again with just a touch of glaze in it, carefully highlighting eye-catching dark brown spots at the tops of the lagoons. Occasionally mark the sides and bottoms of the lagoons as well before softening with just one stroke of the softening brush.

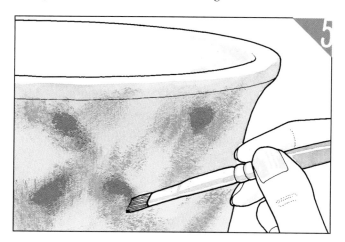

6 The next stage is to soften in all directions with the hog's hair softener – slowly all the colours will move into one another. You can control the degree of yellow in the lagoons by how much brown is softened into them. With such a heavy mix of pigments, you will find that there will inevitably be paint streaks, but they can be removed in the next stage.

7 Use a hakke brush or badger softener for the final softening strokes. This will remove any streaks and help the finished effect to look like real tortoiseshell. Prevent the brush from clogging up with the thick mixture by wiping it continually with a clean piece of kitchen paper (paper towel).

8 Finish off your tortoiseshell item with three or more coats of a polyurethane varnish (see page 12). When dry, rub each coat down with very fine wet-and-dry paper then apply another coat of varnish and sand once more. Finally, rub in a good-quality wax.

Burr Walnut Doors

The mellow, rather grand look of burr walnut combined with elegant antique furniture and dragged walls is ideally suited to the country house look. Here the panelled doors have been painted to harmonize with the wainscoting, and the dragged wall above provides the perfect counterpoint to the patterning of the wood.

Along with bird's eye maple (see pages 94-7) and mahogany, burr walnut has been one of the most popular graining effects for centuries. Real burr walnut is obtained when veneers are sliced from the bumps and protuberances in trees, which can often be seen bulging out of the trunk. In these growths, small branches are trying to grow, and around each of these twigs are growth rings. Just like the main trunk of the tree, as the tree grows the growth rings expand every year but because they are crowded they are forced to grow around one another. This is what creates the interesting, very complicated patterns of the veneer, and this is what you will imitate with paint.

1 Paint the surface in a dark brown eggshell paint. Dissolve some Vandyke Brown crystals in a mixture of half water and half vinegar.

2 The base eggshell coat needs to be degreased so that the water-based glaze you are using will lie evenly over it. Do this by rubbing it with soapy water using a scouring pad until the water lies flat on the surface, and is not breaking up into little patches (a process which is known as cissing).

3 Brush a very light coat of the Vandyke Brown water glaze over the surface and gently mottle it with the wavy mottler and then soften it with the badger softener (see pages 96-7). If you know what patterns you are going to want, you can sweep the mottler around to create the beginnings of heart shapes.

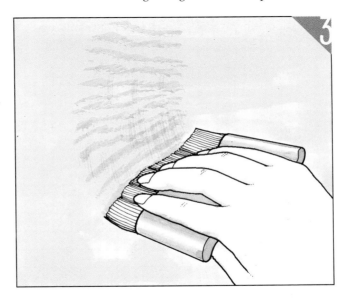

4 Mix the walnut coloured scumble glaze and then combine with a mixture of two volumes of white spirit (mineral spirits) to one volume of boiled linseed oil. The consistency should be similar to thin cream. Brush this lightly all over, using a 5cm (2in) decorator's brush. You will see some of the patterns of the mottling underneath, including some of the heart-shaped patterns if you have attempted them.

5 Mix a little of this glaze into Vandyke Brown oil pigment. Dab a small fitch into it and, after deciding where to position the twigs, place the fitch on the surface and twirl it around between your fingers.

Materials Checklist

- ❊ 5cm (2in) decorator's brush
- ❊ Wavy mottler
- ❊ 7.5cm (3in) badger softener
- ❊ 3–6mm (1/8–1/4in) fitch brush
- ❊ Three-pronged overgrainer
- ❊ 7.5cm (3in) flogging brush
- ❊ Scouring pad
- ❊ Eggshell paint in a dark brown shade
- ❊ Vandyke Brown crystals
- ❊ Vinegar
- ❊ Oil scumble glaze in walnut colour
- ❊ White spirit (mineral spirits)
- ❊ Boiled linseed oil

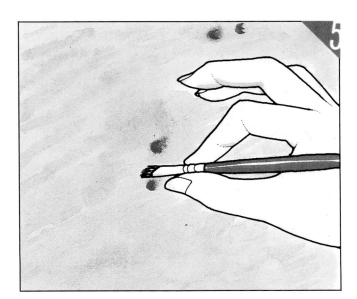

6 Dip the three-pronged overgrainer into the Vandyke Brown pigment and sweep this around the twigs, creating heart shapes. Think about where they will knot into each other and bend and twist.

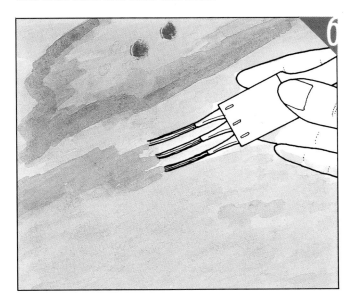

7 Run the wavy mottler around the heart shapes. This will give grain lines of a different fineness to those of the three-pronged overgrainer, adding more variation to the overall pattern.

8 Using a badger softening brush, gently soften the surface, particularly in the heart shapes, softening in an outward direction so that there is a flare on the outside of some of the heart shapes.

9 With the flogging brush, flog the surfaces so that the little ticks you see in the woodgrain appear.

10 Use the small fitch brush and the Vandyke Brown pigment to put in details such as black rings around the heart shapes. Black-in some of the edges of the heart grain to emphasize the overall pattern.

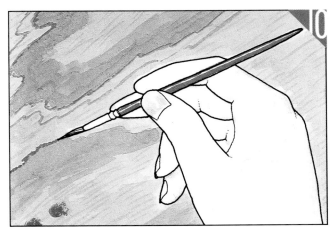

The Neoclassical Style Dining Room

T HE SO-CALLED NEOCLASSICAL PERIOD was in the late eighteenth century, but its origins go back to Classical Greece and Rome. The Renaissance, around the fifteenth century, was seen as a time of rebirth, when classical ideals re-emerged With the Palladian revival of the early eighteenth century, classicism came back into favour, but the full-blown style developed towards the end of the century. It lasted into the nineteenth century, developing into Regency style in England, Empire style in France, Federal and then Empire and Greek Revival in America, and Biedermeier in Germany. By this time there was less ornamentation and a greater simplicity.

Neoclassical interiors reinterpreted the rooms of ancient Greece and Rome. *Trompe l'oeil* columns, murals and garden scenes, as well as plasterwork

and mosaics had featured heavily in Greek and
Roman houses.

Hallmarks of Neoclassical style include classical
motifs such as scrolls, swags and garlands, wreaths,
acanthus and anthemion, medallions, cherubs and the
Greek key border. Winged lions, eagles and sphinxes
appeared in the nineteenth century. In addition,
symmetry and elegance were the watchwords.

Marbling and *trompe l'oeil* urns are closely
associated with Neoclassical style, and the photograph
on pages 30-1 features an interesting combination of the
two. The panelling is first drawn and then fantasy
marbling is carried out by rubbing on a white glaze and
softening across the panels (see pages 48-50). But
whereas this marbling is relatively simple, the *trompe
l'oeil* areas are rather elaborate. Nevertheless, the

principles of highlighting and shading to create a realistic, three-dimensional effect are identical to those used in the much less advanced projects covered in this book (pages 70-1 and 81-3).

The same applies to the complex *trompe l'oeil* work in the photograph on page 32. This not only demonstrates considerable skill but also requires a great deal of training in architectural drawing of columns, mouldings, etc. Yet the shadow effects are still fundamentally the same as those used in the very simple projects in this book.

Another superb example of pure Neoclassicism is the tiny but exquisite dining room shown on the right. Decorated by a skilled mural painter, it was inspired by the Etruscan Dressing Room at Robert Adam's Neoclassical mansion Osterley Park, West London. The light colour above the duck egg blue dado was produced by sponging a light blue onto a parchment ground, using emulsion (latex) glaze mixed with emulsion paint. Acrylic paints in shades of burnt sienna and black were used for the Etruscan vases, sphinxes and dancing maidens, all based on motifs at Osterley. On the cornice (crown molding) and skirting (baseboard), apricot emulsion was wiped onto a stone base, with highlights of burnt sienna. The corridor leading to the dining room is painted to tone with this apricot colour. The painted and distressed chairs are copies of chairs designed by Adam for the Etruscan Dressing Room. Although it would obviously be impossible to achieve as superb an effect as this without the skills of an experienced muralist, you could create a similar look using Neoclassical wallpaper panels and borders, accented by a painted dado and picture rail or cornice.

The paint effect on the wall in the photograph on page 33 (bottom) is easier to achieve. There is no attempt to make the column look three-dimensional, nor is the skirting like real marble, yet the overall effect is delightful. It is done by drawing the outline of the

LEFT: Exquisite mural painting in this room was based upon Neoclassical decoration by Robert Adam.

BELOW: Blatantly false yet still delicate, this trompe l'oeil *column and fantasy marble skirting (baseboard) have great style.*

A limewashed wall and floor provide a mellow, richly textured foil to Neoclassical furnishings in this striking interior.

column on the wall, then stippling the base in a brownish-beige glaze. Yellow ochre is then mixed with the brownish-beige glaze, and this is used for the veins, along with a bluish-grey such as Paynes grey. To create the veins, you simply hold a large pointed brush between thumb and forefinger and drag it along the column in more or less straight lines. Finally, a white glaze is rubbed into the black base of the skirting upon which the column appears to sit. The glaze is then broken up with a pointed brush with a little white spirit (mineral spirits) on it, to allow the black to show through.

The much more rustic effect of the limewashed wood on page 34 provides a wonderful background for the chair. For this, a water glaze containing white acrylic paint is loosely brushed onto the wood to simulate white filler in the woodgrain of the skirting and panelling. On the floor the limewash is brushed over the grey-painted boards, then a rubber graining rocker is pulled through to make it look as though the liming

paste has settled into the grooves of the wood. (The process simulates limed oak, in which furniture makers rub a coloured wax deep into the grain of the oak then wipe it off across the grain, leaving the white liming wax in the grain.)

Of course, paint techniques are not the only way of achieving *trompe l'oeil* effects. The screen, above left, for example, is simply covered with a green textured-effect paper and paper border. The prints and paper "bows" and "chains" are like the print rooms popular in the Neoclassical period. In these, prints were pasted onto the walls and framed by paper trim, rather like those in the photograph above right. The walls were often embellished with cut-out paper ribbons, chains, nails, etc, also pasted onto the walls.

Another, more modern way of decorating the walls with paper is to choose black and white classical wallpaper and borders and create your own panels, as shown on page 36. The look is Neoclassicism brought bang up-to-date.

With the right wallpaper and fabric, it is perfectly possible to create a Neoclassical effect in an otherwise completely plain room.

A very different paper effect which was highly fashionable in the Neoclassical period involved papering the walls with "scenic papers" such as that shown below. These were used continuously all around the room, as here, to form a complete panorama.

However, because they were very expensive, they were sometimes used instead in relatively small panels. The papers are still produced today, and immediately conjure up the Neoclassical period, with its strong affinity for *trompe l'oeil*.

As part of the general fondness for trompe l'oeil *during the Neoclassical period, wallpapers depicting panoramic scenes were popular.*

Leather Effect Wall

This leather effect is a very good imitation of the leather covers of old books, and it can in fact be used on small objects, but it is particularly magnificent on the walls of a dining room. Imagine having dinner by candlelight with the walls reflecting the flickering light like shimmering red leather.

1 Prepare the walls by painting them with a vinyl silk emulsion (latex velvet) in a coral colour. The exact shade is not important as the strength of pigment in the red leather effect will easily cover the emulsion.

2 Make up a fairly thick mixture of crimson and grey oil paints in a ratio of roughly four parts Alizarin Crimson to one part Paynes Grey. This will produce a lovely reddish purple colour. Add a little oil glaze to this. Also, because the crimson dries very slowly, add a few drops of liquid dryer to ensure that the mix will dry overnight.

3 Work on areas of the wall roughly one metre (yard) square at a time. Before applying the crimson mix, cover the area you are working on with a thin layer of transparent oil glaze.

4 Use a domed sash brush to pounce, or dab, on the mix, sometimes applying it slightly thicker to give a darker colour and sometimes a little thinner to give a lighter hue. As this finish is so heavy, your domed sash brush will get very clogged up. Therefore, using one domed sash for the initial pouncing and another for the finer pouncing will be easier. Step back to check that the overall effect will be pleasing to the eye.

Materials Checklist
- ❂ 7.5cm (3in) decorator's brush
- ❂ 1 or 2 domed sash brushes
- ❂ 7.5cm (3in) hog's hair softener
- ❂ 7.5cm (3in) badger hair softener or hakke brush
- ❂ Vinyl silk emulsion (latex velvet) in coral colour
- ❂ Oil paints in Alizarin Crimson and Paynes Grey
- ❂ Oil glaze
- ❂ Liquid dryer

5 Cover the whole wall in patches like this, and link them seamlessly together, again stepping back to take an overall view of the entire wall. Darken areas here and there until the flow of the darker colour into the lighter areas, and vice-versa, gives the impression of a red leather book cover. It might be useful to have such a book by your side so you can refer to it periodically as a guide. Cover the whole wall before going on to the next stage, as the thick mix will dry out slightly, becoming stickier and easier to soften.

6 Soften borders between the light and dark areas and then pounce marks in the crimson mix by gently brushing with a hog's hair softening brush. You will need to continually wipe the brush with a clean piece of kitchen paper (paper towel) to remove excess crimson mix from the brush. The thickness of the mix will mean that you leave marks even when softening.

or a Japanese hakke brush. Carefully skim over the marks left by the hog's hair brush, again cleaning off your brush on kitchen paper (paper towel). With patience, you will be able to make the surface gleam, looking very like a real leather finish. The vinyl silk (latex velvet) base paint may even help you here as the red glaze will settle into pockets in the emulsion (latex) and give darker points which will help to make the whole effect look even more authentic.

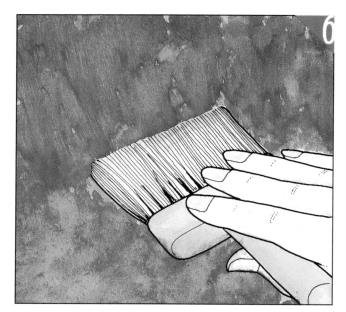

7 Once you have finished softening the whole wall, you will find that the crimson mix is stiffening up, which lends itself well to the final softening process. For this you need either a badger hair softening brush

Gilded Column & Cherub

The delightful variety of objects made in plaster can range from fluted columns and wall brackets like these to ornate baroque mirror frames. Painting and then gilding the plaster creates a dramatic-looking effect that looks good in Neoclassical decor.

The first stage involves sealing the plaster with shellac or French polish, which is made from shellac. Shellac is derived from a resin secreted by the lac beetle and is gathered from bushes in India, then purified and dissolved in alcohol or methylated spirits (denatured alcohol). Shellac can be either clear or slightly brown in colour (when it is called button polish). It can even be stained red or black.

Using the method outlined in step 4 of the gilded column, the liming wax can be mixed with any oil-based pigment to take on any colour you like. This allows you to colour plaster objects to suit your own requirements or decor.

Gilded Column

1 Coat the column with shellac or French polish to seal the plaster. Use an old brush to rapidly coat the surface. The brush will go hard, but it can always be softened up again by cleaning it with methylated spirits. Once the shellac has dried, apply two coats of Black eggshell paint.

2 Make up a glaze consisting of equal parts proprietary oil glaze and Empire Green eggshell paint. A glaze is a thin coat of colour – oil- or water-based – through which you can see a background colour, so be sure not to apply it too thickly. Sponge the glaze onto the column in a loose spiral pattern. When using a sponge, tap it on a piece of lining paper when recharging it to make sure it is not carrying too much glaze. Otherwise, the desired spotty effect produced by the sponge can be lost when the spots all merge together. Continue by lightly sponging the rest of the column before returning to the spiral to add emphasis by making the sponge marks more dense.

3 When the sponged glaze is tacky, float on a little gold powder. This is not real gold, but ground bronze. The easiest way to float the gold onto the column is to place a little on a feather and flick the feather at the column, dusting it on all the way around the spiral.

Materials Checklist
Column:

✿ 5cm (2in) decorator's bush
✿ Marine sponge
✿ Feather
✿ Shellac or French polish (clear)
✿ Eggshell paint in Black and Empire Green
✿ Oil glaze
✿ Bronze powder
✿ Transfer gold leaf or goldsize
✿ Polyurethane varnish
✿ Wax (optional)

4 Next, the rings near the top and base of the column are gilded. This can be done by using gold leaf or bronze powder on goldsize, which is a type of varnish (see page 51). When the goldsize has dried to the tack stage, bronze powder can be dusted on, giving a similar effect to gold or metal leaf; or the leaf can be transferred onto the size from the backing papers on the leaf. Finish with at least three coats of varnish rubbed smooth and, if you wish, waxed.

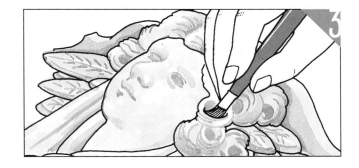

4 Mix oil-based Crimson and Burnt Umber into the liming wax. Rub the brownish-red wax into the wings, and buff up. Now dust the wings lightly with gold powder.

Gilded Cherub Wall Bracket

1 Seal the bracket with the French polish or shellac, as in step 1 of the column. Rub a liming wax into the areas you want to retain a pale look. In this case the face and the two scrolls hanging from it should be waxed. When the wax has dried (this usually takes 10-15 minutes) buff it up with a light dusting cloth.

2 Colour the areas below the face, the acanthus leaves and the bunch of grapes with red shellac and black shellac. Now dust these with a little gold powder, as for the column, step 3.

3 Make the hair of the cherub gold by rubbing in a gold wax. Tap the wax into the crevices and cracks of the hair using a small pointed brush.

5 The gold used in this process, not being real gold leaf, is liable to tarnish. In areas where there is a considerable amount of gold, such as the cherub's hair, it is advisable to finish it off with a coat of varnish.

Materials Checklist Cherub:

❁ *5cm (2in) decorator's brush*
❁ *Shellac or French polish (clear)*
❁ *Liming wax*
❁ *Shellac in red and black*
❁ *Bronze powder*
❁ *Gold wax*
❁ *Oil paints in Crimson and Burnt Umber*
❁ *Polyurethane varnish*

Egyptian Marbled Column & Mirror Frame

Materials Checklist

- ✿ 7.5cm (3in) decorator's brush
- ✿ Fine sponge roller (for column)
- ✿ 7.5cm (3in) hog's hair softener
- ✿ Goose feather
- ✿ Sanding sealer (for mirror frame)
- ✿ Water-based varnish or shellac (for column)
- ✿ Eggshell paint in Black
- ✿ Boiled linseed oil
- ✿ Liquid dryer
- ✿ Oil paints in Oxide of Chromium and White
- ✿ Wax (optional)

Virtually nothing is more suited to a Neoclassical interior than a marbled mirror frame and column. The marbling technique used here – simulating Egyptian green marble – is something beginners can manage, yet it looks surprisingly realistic.

Traditional techniques of marbling simulate true marble with such remarkable accuracy that the methods devised and the brushes developed in Victorian times are still in use today.

Marbling techniques were developed, of course, to save on the huge cost of covering vast areas with enormously expensive stone. Although there is a modern marble from Greece called Tinos which closely resembles Egyptian green marble, it is still a high-cost item. Marbling, like many of the other techniques in this book, can make an object look very expensive at only a fraction of the cost of the real thing. It can be used for either relatively small items or large areas.

The technique shown here is relatively simple, although it does take practice to make it look realistic.

1 Both the mirror frame and the column are made from MDF (medium density fibreboard) and each must be sealed beforehand, using different methods. Seal the mirror frame with a coat of shellac. You can buy this in bottles called sanding sealer, which is shellac mixed with extra additives to give it a stronger finish. Once you have applied a couple of coats and have allowed each to dry thoroughly, rub the wood down with fine wet-and-dry paper until it is smooth and ready for painting. Seal the MDF column with a coat of water-based varnish or, if you wish, shellac.

2 Paint both the mirror frame and the column with at least two coats of Black eggshell. For the column, you will get good results if you apply it using a fine sponge roller. (There will be little drips from the roller, but these can be removed by lightly skimming the surface with a good brush. Any slight brush marks will flow out, leaving a perfectly smooth surface when dry.) For the frame, use a brush. When the paint is dry, rub it down with fine wet-and-dry paper until the surface is totally smooth.

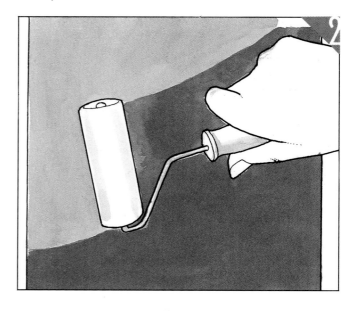

3 Make up a glaze of boiled linseed oil and add to it a couple of drops of a dryer, an agent which causes oil-based materials to dry overnight. Add a couple of drops of dryer to the artist's oil colour Oxide of Chromium, too. (Unless the drying agent is added to these two materials, neither the glaze nor the pigment will be dry the following day.) Using a brush or a rag, apply a coat of the linseed oil glaze over the entire surface of the mirror frame or column.

4 Cut a feather with a pair of scissors to give it a long serrated edge. To ensure that the tips of the serrations are fairly fine, cut a straight edge down the feather first, about 1.2cm (1/2in) from the spine. Any closer to the spine and the feather is too thick.

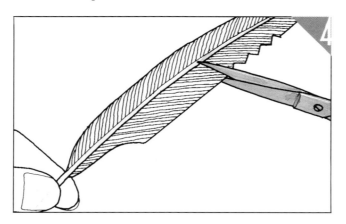

5 Spread the Oxide of Chromium out on a palette and dip the serrated tips of the feather into it, wiping these again on the palette to make sure that the feather is not too heavily coated. Touch the surface of the mirror frame or column with the feather to lay on tiny green dots, making the dots form clusters in a slanting design and leaving clear black random patches, like lagoons. (A quick way of creating more densely dotted areas is to dip a piece of plastic pot-scourer into the oil colour and tap this gently onto the surface.)

6 When the dots are dry, apply another coat of linseed oil glaze. This adds the appearance of depth so that you seem to see below the surface, as with real marble.

7 Add a touch of White to the Oxide of Chromium. Do not mix them together thoroughly, as you want a streaky effect. Using the feather, trickle this slightly lighter green through the original dots in little squiggles, like water trickling between grains of sand on a beach. These squiggles represent the veining in the marble. They can be dense in some areas and lighter in others and can even travel across some of the black lagoons. You can only judge if the effect is building up to your liking by stepping back now and again to see whether the mixture of dots, light squiggles, dark squiggles and

black lagoons looks right. There are now two layers of colour and the marbling is starting to take on a feeling of depth, with the lighter greens at the surface and the darker dots looking as though they are set much deeper. Once the squiggles are dry you can proceed to the next stage.

8 The white mineral quartz tends to find its way into marble. The easiest way to simulate it is to mix up a range of colours, from a very white green (White with a

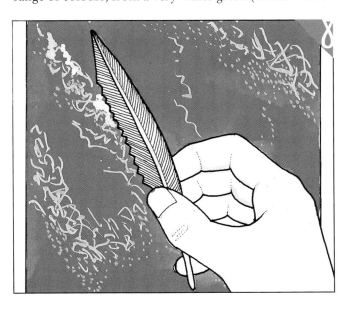

little Oxide of Chromium added) to a pure White pigment. To each of your colours you must add a drop of dryer. There is no need to apply an oil glaze to the surface this time as you don't want the white to smear. Apply the white pigments with the feather in a series of dots as before. Follow the general direction of the slanting design you have created and imagine that the quartz is trying to trickle across the surface.

9 Apply more dots where there are the most squiggles and then soften them with a hog's hair softening brush. As the dots are fairly light and there is no oil on the surface, the white will not spread out too much and will begin to look as though it is actually inset into the surface of a marble stone. Occasionally, instead of dotting, you can allow the feather to run a little vein through the green marble, sometimes into or along the edge of the "lagoons". This gives a very realistic final finish to the marble.

10 Varnish the mirror frame and column very carefully (see page 12) with at least three coats of varnish, to give it the hard, shiny look of marble. If a waxy look is preferred, rub the final coat down with wet-and-dry paper, wax it and then buff it up.

Fantasy Marbling

Though eclectically furnished, this dramatic room has a Neoclassical feel because of the air of grandeur the marbling of the woodwork produces. This type of marbling – sometimes known as marbleizing – gives a decorative effect with the impression of real marble while not attempting to simulate the real thing. It is, in other words, a fantasy marble.

The method of creating veins in this marbling technique requires a great deal of skill and patience but it is the professional method of veining. Although this is a fantasy marble technique, the same principles can be used in *trompe l'oeil* simulations of complicated marbles. There are simpler methods of creating fantasy marbles, and veins can be created by trickling feathers through the background you have created (see pages 46-7). Feathers, however, are only really effective on small-scale projects as they become damaged; they cannot give repetitive patterns on larger surfaces such as a series of panels. It is, therefore, worth persevering to master this veining technique.

The marble should be based on two colours – either two colours from the warm range (red, orange, yellow) or two from the cool range (greens and blues). One must be lighter than the other.

Materials Checklist

- ✿ 7.5cm (3in) decorator's brush
- ✿ Domed sash brush
- ✿ 7.5cm (3in) hog's hair softener
- ✿ 1.2cm (1/2in) fitch brush
- ✿ Small, pointed brush (such as a swordliner or a sable artist's brush)
- ✿ Eggshell paint in White
- ✿ Oil glaze
- ✿ Oil paints in two warm or two cool shades
- ✿ White spirit (mineral spirits)
- ✿ Polyurethane varnish

1 Paint the surface with at least two coats of White eggshell paint, rubbing each coat down once it is dry with a fine wet-and-dry paper, as described on page 51.

2 Rub on a very thin skin of transparent oil glaze. This will act like a kind of skating rink for the marbling colours so that when they are softened, they gently even out over the surface.

3 Add a very small amount of the transparent oil glaze to each of the colours you are using and mash it up with a palette knife to make the pigment easier to use. Imagine that the mineral in the marble represented by the lighter colour is going to flow over the surface like the sea over sand, leaving some patches bare and other patches covered with water. Using a domed sash brush, start the first wave of lighter colour at the top of the panel and work at a slanting angle towards the bottom. Tap the colour on with the domed sash, brushing irregularly using the top and the sides of the brush as well as spinning and rubbing it so that the marks are almost entirely random.

4 Move a little way along the wall, again starting at the top, and mark on another flow at an angle from top to bottom, allowing this one to merge in places with the first. Try always to have a general slanting direction of flow, otherwise it will be too complicated trying to work out the flow direction of each area.

5 Once you have covered the panel with these flows, gently soften them with a hog's hair softening brush, first in the direction of the flow and then across the flow to remove any brush marks.

6 There are two problems you may encounter at this stage. If you have tapped the pouncing brush too regularly, you may end up with a series of little round marks. And if you tense up so that you do not achieve a flowing motion, you will create a series of round marks in a wiggly chain, like worms. The trick is to pounce and rub the brush so all the marks fade into one another.

7 The next stage involves the use of a fitch brush. When using this, put very little colour on it, then tap it on the palette paper so it's not too heavily loaded. Tap in the darker colour along one of the edges of the flows but do not follow the flow all the way to the bottom of the panel. Now move along to another edge, beginning slightly further down the panel. Repeat this process to create a series of leading edges staggered around the piece you are marbling. Pounce the leading edges back into the lighter colour as if the two minerals represented by the colours are blending into one another. The darker colour will merge but it will always be darkest along the original leading edges.

8 Soften the darker colour effect with the hog's hair, working first in the direction of the flow and then at right angles to it.

9 Now you can start breaking up the overall effect to give more interesting patterns. Using a piece of crumpled paper, tap and scrub into the surface in the direction of the flow, creating little broken marks. Soften these with the hog's hair to create a pleasing effect. Some of the leading edges can be sharpened up using bits of paper, and a little of either the lighter or the darker colour can be tapped into the white patches to make them look more natural.

10 The most difficult part of this procedure is creating veins. For this you will need to use a pointed brush. Pick the brush up and roll it between your first finger and thumb. This is the motion you need to use when creating the veins. Using the darker edges as a guide, roll a vein across the panel from one dark edge through to another in sharp jagged lines. Work in the general direction of the flow, creating two or three dark main veins crossing your piece. Twiddle the brush slightly to the left when you are moving left and twiddle it slightly to the right when you are moving

right. This helps to make the veins look natural and to keep the point on the brush.

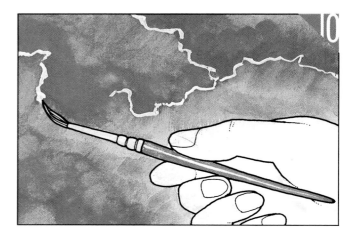

11 Soften the veins you have just made, mostly in the direction of the flow. If you try to soften these crosswise too much, they will spread out, and you need these veins to remain as thin as possible.

12 Now start creating the secondary veins, which lead into the main veins. Again move in the direction of the flow. By the time you have softened these, they will probably have the same depth of colour as the main veins. Therefore, go back over the main veins, creating the occasional darker tone so that they stand out beside the lighter veins and create a feeling of depth in the surface of the marble.

13 The final trick is to take another brush with a little bit of white spirit (mineral spirits) on it, splatter it very slightly onto the surface so you cannot even see the white spirit then gently soften with the hog's hair. Little teardrop shapes will appear. Although a fantasy effect, it will look very convincing.

14 Varnish the marbled surface with at least three coats of varnish (see page 12), rubbing it down using wet-and-dry paper in the usual way.

Gilded Frames

Gilded mirror or picture frames look wonderful in any traditional style of decor, particularly Neoclassical. Although they are expensive to buy, you can gild an old frame yourself using the technique shown here.

Gilding – the process of applying gold, silver, bronze or other metal powders or leaves to a surface – has been practised for centuries. The technique of gilding using transfer silver, gold or bronze leaf gives a richer, more lustrous finish than you will achieve using bronze powder or metallic paint. There are two main processes used: oil gilding and water gilding. Oil gilding, a relatively simple technique, is used here.

Water gilding is much more difficult. It requires a surface so smooth that when the gold leaf is applied and rubbed with a special tool called an agate, the gold can be made to gleam. If, however, the surface is even the slightest bit rough, rubbing with the auger will tear open the gold leaf. To achieve the ultra-smooth surface involves building up several layers of different materials including gesso, a mixture of rabbit skin glue and a chalk substance called whiting. On top of this are spread even smoother layers of a fine clay called bole, which comes in a variety of colours, the most common being a reddish brown. Water gilding is, therefore, a long and laborious process which is best left to the experts. With oil gilding, on the other hand, you can achieve good results even as a beginner.

With the oil gilding process, you cannot simulate the highly burnished gleam obtained in the water gilding method, but, at any rate, this would only be required on a restoration job. What is more frequently desired is the look of old silver or gold leaf, and for this the method shown here works extremely well.

1 Begin by painting on two coats of reddish brown eggshell paint; when brushed on well, this will flow out to leave no brush marks. Rub down the final coat of eggshell with a very fine wet-and-dry paper. The surface of the subject must be wetted as well as the paper and then rubbed completely smooth so that when you touch it with your fingertips there is no feeling of grit.

2 Next, apply the goldsize. This is a kind of varnish onto which the gold leaf will later be laid. In traditional oil-based gilding, oil-based sizes are used. These are designated as 1 hour, 3 hour and 24 hour sizes, which refer to the time it takes for each of the different sizes to dry to the point at which perfect gilding could be achieved. If the leaf is put on too soon, it will crinkle; too late and it will fail to adhere to the surface. For perfect gilding, the size has to reach tack"point. (The tack point can be recognized by rubbing the back of your finger over the size – it should produce a slight squeaking noise.) Today, however, it is possible to speed up this process using a relatively new product – a water-based size which takes only about 15 minutes to reach tack point. It is painted onto the smoothed-down eggshell in as thin and smooth a coating as possible, then left to tack.

3 The metal leaf – either transfer silver or transfer bronze (the bronze, which is known as Dutch metal, simulates real gold leaf) – is laid over the goldsize once tack point is reached. Rub the backing paper gently with cotton wool (cotton balls) and then carefully peel the paper away to leave the metal leaf on the frame.

Materials Checklist

- ✪ 5cm (2in) decorator's brush
- ✪ Eggshell paint in a reddish brown shade
- ✪ Oil- or water-based goldsize
- ✪ Transfer silver or transfer bronze leaf (known as Dutch metal)
- ✪ Cotton wool (cotton balls)
- ✪ Rotten-stone (optional)
- ✪ Oil paint in Raw Umber mixed with white spirit (mineral spirits) (optional)
- ✪ Varnish

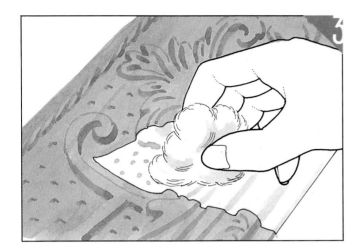

the red eggshell paint behind the leaf, simulating the way the reddish-brown bole shows through damaged gold or silver leaf that has been applied with the water gilding process.

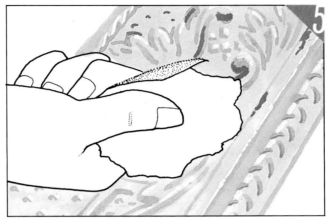

4 Getting the leaf into the deep cracks and crevices of the frame can be a real problem. To overcome this, take a brush with a loose head of bristle, and dust silver powder or simulated gold (ie bronze) powder into the crevices. Brush off any loose powder with a clean brush, which at the same time will burnish the metal leaf, and the entire surface will look as though it has been gilded.

6 Another trick can be used in antiquing the gold to make it look as though it has aged. Gold is an inert metal and, unlike copper or bronze, does not tarnish or react with other chemicals, but it does get dirty. Therefore, to simulate a few years' dirt you can mix up a paste of Raw Umber and white spirit (mineral spirits). Push this into the cracks and crevices, brushing it all over the frame, and then rub it off with a cloth, leaving behind just enough here and there to give a realistic appearance of age.

7 You can also achieve an antique effect by dusting the frame with a powdered stone called rotten-stone. Push it into the cracks to look like dust, completing the appearance of an aged and time-worn picture frame. Be sure to wear a mask – you must not breathe in the rotten-stone powder.

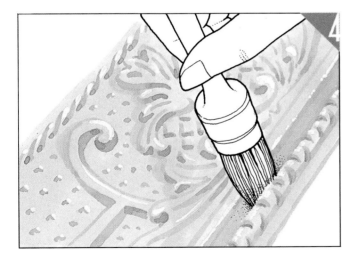

5 The next stage is to make the silver or gold look old. Distressing the surface involves physically damaging the metal leaf by hitting it with a bunch of keys or rubbing it with some rough sandpaper. This will expose

8 Unlike real gold, bronze metal leaf will tarnish, so to prevent this give it a coat of varnish (see page 12). Allow the varnish to dry before tapping the rotten-stone into the cracks.

White Marbled Walls

Architectural prints displayed on a white marbled wall flanked by marbled pilasters create a Neoclassical effect in this room. Real marble comes in many colours and patterns, including black, pink, green and white. Even white marble can vary enormously in colour, ranging from types with yellow veins through green or blue-grey veins to black veins. The marbling shown here simulates white marble with yellow veins. As mentioned on page 48, this method of veining is quite difficult. Nevertheless, it is the way professionals create realistic veins and so is worth persevering with.

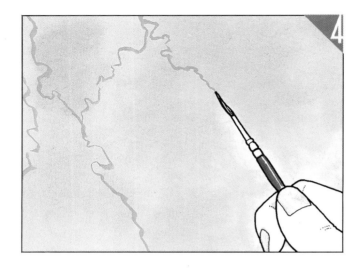

1 Paint the surface with at least two coats of White eggshell, rubbing each coat down when it is dry with a fine wet-and-dry paper, as described on page 51.

as described on page 51.

2 Mix the oil glaze with Yellow Ochre and a touch of Paynes Grey. Using crumpled paper or a cloth, rub this gently over the surface, starting at the top and working at a slanting angle towards the bottom. Move along the wall, again starting at the top, and apply another flow at an angle from top to bottom, allowing this one to merge in places with the first. Try always to have a general slanting direction of working.

3 Brush out and then soften this with a hog's hair softener, until you have the faintly dappled background colour shown in the photograph.

4 Take the pointed brush and, holding it between your thumb and forefinger, roll it across the surface in sharp, jagged lines to create a vein. (For more about painting in veins, see page 50.)

5 Make more veins in the same way. The brush will get clogged up, so dissolve the build-up in white spirit (mineral spirits), wipe the point of the brush clear, put some more of the pigment on the brush, and carry on.

6 The next stage is to soften the veins in their direction of flow. Use the hog's hair softener in the direction of flow to first remove some of the wetness and then very gently brush from side to side. This will prevent them from spreading out too much.

7 To make the veins look more three-dimensional and realistic, take up some more of the pigment on the pointed brush, and darken parts of the veins.

8 To create the effect of white veins, put a little white spirit on the pointed brush and drag it through the hazy glaze to reveal the white background. Soften these veins too with the hog's hair softener.

Materials Checklist

- ✿ 7.5cm (3in) decorator's brush
- ✿ 7.5cm (3in) hog's hair softener
- ✿ Small, pointed brush (such as a swordliner or a sable artist's brush)
- ✿ Eggshell paint in White
- ✿ Oil glaze
- ✿ Oil paints in Yellow Ochre and Paynes Grey
- ✿ White spirit (mineral spirits)

The Gustavian Style Hall

GUSTAVIAN STYLE refers to the elegant homes of wealthy Swedes of the late eighteenth century, during the reign of King Gustav III. Cool, restrained and elegant, it is simultaneously simple and sophisticated – and utterly delightful.

One reason for its distinctive look is the Gustavian palette, in which cool blue, pearl grey and straw yellow, as well as washed-out peach and a very dusky pink, predominate. Tall windows, pale faded walls, bleached floorboards, painted wooden furniture and simple furnishing fabrics such as checks and stripes all made the rooms light and airy.

Classical symmetry was important in Gustavian style, so much so that the tall, columnar tiled stoves which heated Swedish rooms were often duplicated with a *faux* wood version, to preserve the symmetry of the room, as in the photograph on the right.

These stoves featured heavily in Gustavian rooms, and the wonderful colours of the gleaming tiles echo the soft blue-greys and straw colours of the decor, as the photograph on page 58 shows. The straight-legged

wooden chairs popular at the time were often painted *en suite* with the panelling behind them, as can be seen in the same photograph.

Another distinctive element of Gustavian style was the discreet use of sparkling crystal and gilt, in the form of crystal chandeliers, gilt mirrors and other restrained touches of gilt in the painting. The room on page 61 is a good example of this.

For an authentic look it's important for the gilding to be subtle. For example, to achieve an effect similar to the cherub on page 60 (left) rub in a glaze, and then use your fingertip to rub in a gilt varnish, giving the appearance of an old statue that has been gilded in places, of which only small amounts have been left behind.

The bow at the top of the gilt mirror on page 61 is typical of Gustavian mirrors and illustrates one of the most charming aspects of Gustavian style – its unique blending of the Neoclassical with the rococo. Rococo had been the predominant style of the mid-eighteenth century in Europe but had largely been replaced by Neoclassicism by the late eighteenth century when Gustavian style emerged. However, in Sweden rococo lingered for a little longer, and the lighthearted, slightly whimsical touches it engendered served to soften the severity of Neoclassicism.

The best-known feature of Gustavian interiors is probably the wonderful hand-painted decoration on the walls, as in the photographs on page 62 and right. Used instead of the silk wall coverings fashionable elsewhere in the late eighteenth century, the panels were often painted onto stretched canvas fixed above the painted wainscot. As well as borders and garlands of flowers or foliage, as shown in those photographs, rosettes and portrait medallions, posies of flowers, bows, columns and urns were all popular – again, a charming mixture of the Neoclassical and the rococo. The colours here too were the lovely muted blue-greys and soft straw yellows that featured so heavily in Gustavian decor.

Sometimes the painting was fairly simple, as in the room shown on page 61 while in other cases it could be highly finished or even quite theatrical, as on page 60 (right). The use of gilt, as here, gave a beautiful lift to the soft, chalky paint.

PRECEDING SPREAD, OPPOSITE AND ABOVE: Hand-painted wall decoration was a hallmark of Gustavian style.

*BELOW LEFT,
BELOW RIGHT
AND OPPOSITE:
Muted colours
enlivened by gilt
characterized
Gustavian style.*

Today, to create a similar effect such as that on page 62, you can apply two or three colours of a modern distemper (calcimine), rub them through (see pages 121-3) and then rub over a slightly darker-toned glaze. A frieze could be stencilled and then rubbed through to make it look as aged as the wall.

Similarly, to achieve the effect of the statue and surrounding decoration shown on page 59, create an effect of age using touches of white emulsion (latex) paint in protruding areas, and a darker colour in the shadows. The frieze around the niche can be pencilled in loosely. To do this, draw the flowers on tracing paper, then pencil on the reverse side of the paper using a soft pencil, and place the tracing on the walls. Draw around the design on the front of the tracing paper and the pencil on the reverse side will be transferred, leaving a faint trace of the design on the wall. The flowers can then be painted in freehand.

Walls and furniture painted in blue-greys and straw yellows contributed to the look of understated elegance so characteristic of Gustavian interiors.

Sky Ceiling

Painted sky ceilings were fashionable in Sweden (as elsewhere) in the late eighteenth and early nineteenth centuries. They are very effective examples of *trompe l'oeil*, especially in a room with a high ceiling where the details of the painting are less obvious. In true *trompe l'oeil* style, they "deceive the eye" to make it seem like one is looking up at the sky.

The technique used in this project will produce the effect of a simple, cloudy summer sky. If you study the storm clouds of a Constable painting, however, or the sunsets and sunrises of Turner, you will find that by using more elaborate versions of this technique you can produce much more dramatic skies.

It is essential in creating a convincing sky that you take a look at what you have done from the ground to make sure that you are achieving the right effect. This is fairly easy if you are working on a ladder, but if you have to use a scaffolding tower to reach the ceiling, it is helpful to have someone on the ground who can watch your work progressing. They can then tap the ceiling with a stick to point out where there needs to be, say, more white for a high point, or more grey to get the base of the cloud correct.

1 Paint the ceiling with an appropriate sky blue emulsion (latex) paint. This will form the sky background showing through the clouds.

2 Make up a white water-based glaze for the thinner clouds by mixing a little White with the glaze and adding a touch of Yellow Ochre. Clouds tend to have a slightly off-white colour due to the sun shining above them. Then, using a sponge, simply wipe the glaze across the sky, tapping it roughly with scrunched-up balls of paper and spreading the glaze out by brushing backwards and forwards with a good-quality brush. This will produce the effect of the light, wispy clouds you see high up in the sky.

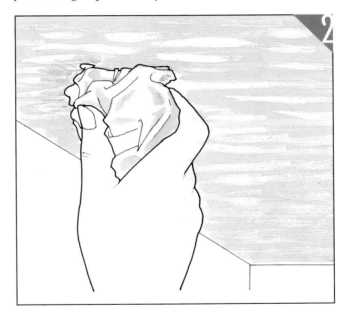

3 Take a look at the overall effect of the wispy clouds and decide which you can develop into the billowing cumulus clouds you see on a hot summer's day. Select a cloud and, applying the glaze with the sponge, rub a billowing effect inside the edge of the wispy cloud, making the inner part (the front of the cloud) heaviest and keeping it lighter towards the outside (the back of the cloud). Again use scrunched-up paper to roughly tap the edges. Soften the edges with a brush so that some of the edges become faint or spread out like little wisps into the blue of the sky.

Materials Checklist
- ❂ 7.5cm (3in) decorator's brush
- ❂ Fitch brush
- ❂ Marine sponge
- ❂ Emulsion (latex) paint in a sky blue shade
- ❂ Water-based glaze
- ❂ Acrylic paints in White, Yellow Ochre, Black and Ultramarine (optional)

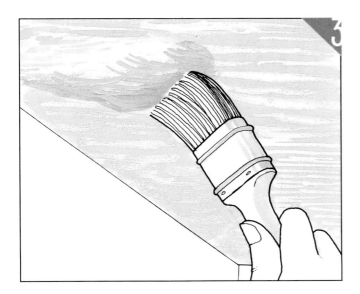

7 Stand back and examine the whole cloud and decide which areas might look better with a slightly warmer white. Using the brush, touch in areas of white with Yellow Ochre where required. You will always have to use your own judgement in deciding what looks right, but it is a good idea to have to hand a photograph of the sky or an image of a Constable painting as a guide.

8 Now study the overall effect that you have created: the high points in white, the mid tones with the slightly yellowish white, and the different shades of grey in the base of the clouds. You might think that some of the clouds, or some parts of them, do not have the correct shape, or maybe an outside edge looks a bit odd. You might want to split a cloud by having part of it dissolving away. To make alterations, make up a glaze using the original sky blue emulsion and, with a fitch brush, use this to paint out any areas of cloud with which you are not happy. Also, if you want to create areas of the sky which are a deeper blue, so that you have a mixture of a deep blue sky behind some clouds and a lighter blue behind others, put a little Ultramarine acrylic paint into the mix. Again, a photograph or a picture of a painting showing a sky can be used as a guide.

4 When this cloud looks right, repeat the process in other areas of the sky, creating smaller and larger versions of the cloud you have just made and building up the basis for a summer's day cloud pattern.

5 The inner part of the cloud is usually slightly more grey as the sunlight has not penetrated through the denser part of the cloud. Make a grey glaze by adding a little Black to the white glaze. (You can also experiment with different greys by using red and blue to give a purple tinge or even a touch of green. There are more colours in a cloudy sky than you might at first think.) Sponge on the grey mixture to create the billowing interior of the cloud in the same way that the outer edge was developed. Again, tap with paper and soften until the cloud takes on the desired form.

6 The next stage is to emphasize the sun catching the top of the clouds. You need to have more control over the spread of the glaze for this, so use a brush to apply the off-white glaze. Brush it onto the edges of the clouds that you judge would be the highest. Use some pure white glaze at times to highlight the areas that would pick up the most direct sunlight.

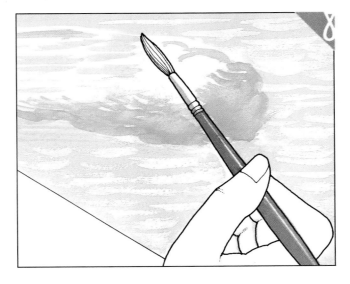

Gustavian Style Furniture

Gustavian interiors were based on soft pastel colours, which are well represented nowadays by the modern versions of distemper (calcimine) paints. These give a beautifully soft, powdery effect. When dry, they are easily rubbed through with sandpaper, which means that they can be antiqued and distressed.

Distemper is used here on a Swedish blanket chest, a chair (shown on page 71) and a coatstand. The angel medallion on the chest is painted in by hand.

Blanket chest

1 Paint the entire chest with emulsion (latex) paint. Use white all over except for the back rest, which should be a sky blue.

2 Once the emulsion is dry, paint a deep yellow distemper paint over the white base. When it has also dried, sand it so that some of the white reappears.

3 Now paint a lighter yellow, made from equal parts Deep Yellow and White, over the entire box except for the blue medallion. When dry, rub this through using a mixture of coarse, medium and fine wet-and-dry papers. The rougher paper is used in the areas where you would see more wear-and-tear, and the gentle final rub-down with the very fine wet-and-dry paper gives a lovely silky feeling to the surface.

4 The front panel of the seat is given a combed finish. First make up a water-based glaze using the yellow distemper mixed into a proprietary water glaze. Brush this on all over and comb through with a rubber comb.

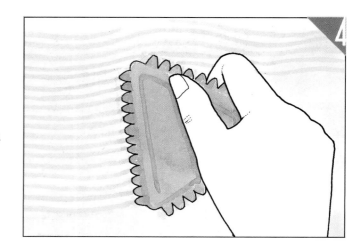

5 The sides around the combed panel are given a wavy decorative border in blue. Mix some of the sky blue emulsion into the water glaze, using a thin mix, like watercolour, so that the final version has an "old" look. The technique is very simple. Take a brush with a nice bulbous tip, and as soon as you start brushing, press harder and harder so that the brush head progressively flattens out, spreading the blue quite wide. Then lift off slowly so that the brush head contracts, thinning out the blue colour. At the same time you should move the brush up and down in a curve.

6 When the blue is dry, rub the sides with a fine wet-and-dry paper to make it seem as though the wavy border has faded into the surface, giving an aged, distressed look as if worn by years of use.

7 Next, lightly draw a circle with a scalloped edge inside the medallion. Paint the inner part with sky blue emulsion, and outside with the light yellow you

used elsewhere. Find a suitable picture of an angel, and copy it onto tracing paper, enlarging or reducing it first on a photocopier if necessary. Rub the back of the tracing paper with a graphite pencil, and then lay the paper over the medallion so that the design can be traced onto the blue. To prevent any pencil marks dirtying the surface, spray the blue medallion with fixative and allow it to dry before transferring the tracing onto the surface.

8 The following oil colours will be required for the angel: Naples Yellow, Yellow Ochre, Cerulean Blue, Raw Umber and White. Each must be mixed in with an oil glaze. It is also possible to work with acrylic colours of the same name mixed into water glazes. If you practise painting the angel a number of times before starting on the blanket chest, you will begin to get a feel of how to copy simple pictures like this from illustrations and begin the process which may lead to mural work.

9 Add a little White to the Naples Yellow and mix it into the glaze until it is almost a watercolour consistency. Brush this freely over all the flesh tones, the face and the body.

10 Add a little of the Cerulean Blue to the preceding colour and use it to paint the wings.

11 The features on the face are painted in next. Add a spot of White to a little Raw Umber glaze, and use this to paint in the eyebrows. Also use it around the eyes, nose and mouth. Paint in the whites of the eyes with White and finally use Cerulean Blue for the pupils. Highlight each pupil with a tiny dot of White. Fill in the mouth with a pink colour, made from a mix of Cadmium Red and White. On the lower lip, which is usually lighter, rub in a touch more white. Paint around the scalloped edge with Yellow Ochre.

12 Make up a stronger greenish/blue colour than the previous one (step 10) and loosely brush this across the wings to indicate the shadows of the feathers.

13 Add a little blue to the original Naples Yellow and White and brush this into the shadowy areas of the face and body.

14 For the hair the original Naples Yellow and White is loosely brushed over the area. Then a darker mix, using some Raw Umber, is painted on in little wiggly lines to indicate the shadows of the curls. Use a little extra White in the Naples Yellow mix to touch in some highlights on the curls. Finally, paint the halo using a yellow colour.

15 The clouds at the bottom are simply sponged on using a little White to give the general feel of a cloud. (See page 111 for details of sponging.)

Wooden chair

The chair is painted in a similar way to the blanket chest (steps 1-6), but using a lighter yellow on top of the white base. When it is dry, rub it through to give a feeling of age. To get even more of an antique feel, apply the darker yellow to areas where you would expect the dirt of ageing – the tops and bottoms of the back rungs of the chair, and the tops and bottoms of the legs and spindles. Using a little fitch brush, blend these darker areas out into the lighter yellow, tapering them off.

Coatstand

This should be treated similarly to the chair – it should be painted white; then painted a light yellow; next, rubbed through; then darker areas added to indicate ageing. You can also use touches of gold, as sometimes seen on Scandinavian furniture. You might like to add these to the tops of the coat-hanging struts and to the ring in the middle of the coatstand simply by rubbing in a gold wax.

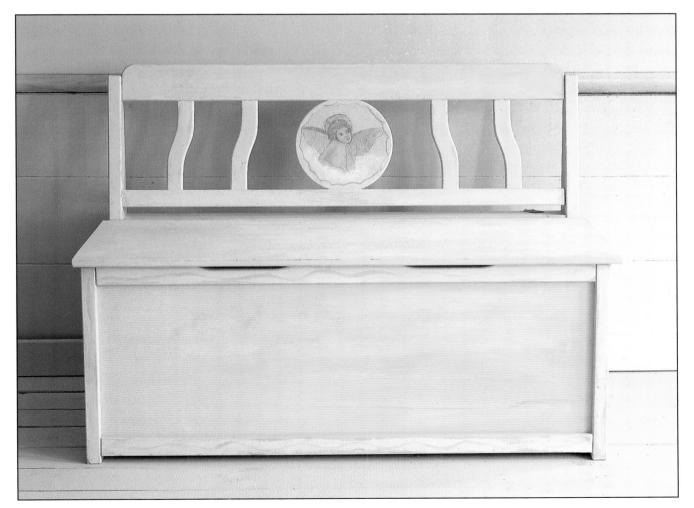

Gustavian Wall

Here is an easy way to create the light, muted walls of a Gustavian interior. The *trompe l'oeil* chair rail and horizontal cladding effects add interest and prevent the wall from looking too flat. Instructions for painting the chair are given on page 69.

1 First paint the wall a pale grey using either Pearl or Portland Grey emulsion (latex). Once this is dry, mark the position of the *trompe l'oeil* chair rail and planks of wood cladding using a pencil, a straightedge and a spirit level (carpenter's level) to ensure that they are all horizontal.

2 Make up a water glaze using the Pearl or Portland Grey and add to it a little Black acrylic and a little Raw Umber so that it is slightly darker than the grey of the wall. Paint this mix evenly over the area beneath the top pencil line. Now, while the paint is still wet, drag a dragging brush or varnishing brush through the glaze from side to side, to create the effect of wood that has been painted with a grey lime wash. Drag the chair rail and the three cladding planks separately.

3 Once the glaze has dried you can move on to creating the false shadow. Apply two strips of masking tape, one running outside the top pencil line and one along the inside of the line at the bottom. Then, using a grey oil crayon slightly darker than the grey of the simulated wood, draw a line along the edge of the top tape and of the bottom tape. Loosen up the crayon line using a tiny brush with some white spirit (mineral spirits) and/or oil glaze on it, softening the line in towards the centre of the chair rail. Finally, soften with

a fitch brush, creating a line which is slightly darker at the edge and fades in towards the centre of the rail, and which is slightly stronger beneath than on top. This imitates the effect of light hitting the top of the chair rail. Use an oil crayon in a slightly darker grey and apply a narrow band along the bottom line of the chair rail, fading it off into the top plank of cladding. This represents the shadow of the rail on the wall.

4 Using a white crayon, create a highlight by applying a band of white along the part of the chair rail onto which you feel the light would fall. Rub this line with your finger so that it no longer looks like a crayon line and it becomes simply a band of soft white light along the chair rail.

5 Select another crayon darker than the grey of the lime-washed planks and apply a thin line beneath each plank to look like a shadow. Below this line draw an even thinner line of white. These lines will represent the light hitting the higher plank, casting a shadow under its bottom edge and then highlighting the top edge of the plank below.

Materials Checklist

- ✿ 7.5cm (3in) decorator's brush
- ✿ 7.5cm (3in) dragging or varnishing brush
- ✿ Tiny artist's brush
- ✿ Fitch brush
- ✿ Emulsion (latex) paint in Pearl Grey or Portland Grey
- ✿ Water glaze
- ✿ Acrylic paint in Black and Raw Umber
- ✿ Oil crayons in White and 3 shades of grey
- ✿ White spirit (mineral spirits) and/or oil glaze

The Provencal Style Kitchen

WHEREAS THE HEART of the English country house is the drawing room, the heart of the French home is the kitchen, and nowhere more so than in Provence. The kitchens are practical, unfussy and unpretentious, with an emphasis on serious food preparation and eating. Food is the focal point here.

For an instant Provencal flavour that is relatively inexpensive, use a *banquette,* or wooden two-seater settee, for your kitchen seating. On the one which is shown in the photograph on the right, the paintwork is an aged-looking distemper or emulsion (latex). Bands of other colours, simple stencilling on the back, and carving picked out in the green and red colours, all well-aged, add character and interest to this piece. The picture demonstrates that the ageing technique (see

pages 121-3) is well suited not only to panelling but also to freestanding pieces of furniture.

The colourwashing technique – as explained in the project on pages 84-5 – used on the yellow wall behind the *banquette* is ideally suited to kitchen walls in a Provencal style kitchen. Other examples are the kitchens on the left and on page 80, in which emulsion (latex) glazes have been used to create soft terracotta and ochre-yellow colourwashed walls. These warm, earthy shades are very evocative of Provence and the South of France.

On the walls of the kitchen in the photographs on pages 76 and 77, the reddish-pink old plastered wall was created in much the same way. The cupboards too have an aged appearance. To achieve this sort of effect, use multiple layers of distemper (calcimine), combined with stencilled flowers, rubbing the surface of both to resemble old paintwork.

Bright splashes of colour look wonderful against a background of walls colourwashed in soft mustard, honey, apricot, rose or terracotta. Glazed Provencal pottery in rich yellows and greens, for example, is perfect. The distinctive Provencal cotton fabrics with their bright, small-scale prints look wonderful as squab cushions, simple curtains or table linen. For other colour accents, you cannot do better than the Provencal produce itself – flowers such as mimosa, geraniums and sunflowers, bunches of lavender and piles of colourful vegetables and citrus fruits.

Aged-looking paint looks good on furniture here, as in the kitchens on pages 78 and also 79. An *armoire* – either genuine or copied for kitchen units – epitomizes French country style probably more than any other piece of furniture. It will prove invaluable in the kitchen (as in other rooms), since it can be used to hold anything from preserves to china to Provencal print tablecloths and napkins. If the contents are interesting enough, and the insides as well as the outsides of the doors painted, the *armoire* can be left permanently open.

PRECEDING SPREAD: The rush-seated banquette *not only introduces a Provencal element into the kitchen but also provides an opportunity to display stencilling or hand-painting skills.*

LEFT: A terracotta colourwash provides a soft background for stronger colours in this kitchen.

Here, a built-in dresser has been given a treatment similar to that of the walls of the adjacent kitchen. The stencilling too has been rubbed back to make it look as aged as the rest of the surfaces.

Near the *armoire* in the Provencal kitchen, chairs will be gathered around a sturdy wooden table, its top either plain and well-scrubbed or covered with tiles or oilcloth. This is used by family and friends for all meals that aren't taken *al fresco.*

In addition to the *armoire* and *banquette*, other pieces traditionally found in the Provencal kitchen include the

pétrin, a chest used for preparing bread dough; the carved wood *panetière*, which hangs on the wall to hold baguettes; and the *salière*, a salt box with a hinged lid.

Apart from colourwashed walls and ceilings, the floor is another surface that will need thoughtful treatment if you want to attain a French Provincial look. Flagstones are often found in rural French

On the walls of this kitchen, layers of chalky distemper (calcimine) paint have been rubbed back to create a time-worn look.

A splendid painted armoire holds pride of place in this kitchen's eating area.

kitchens, but if you don't happen to have them in your house, you might wish to fake them, as in the project on pages 81-3.

Terracotta tiles are also often found on Provencal kitchen floors. Locally fired tiles – white or coloured, and plain or simply patterned – are frequently used on walls, work surfaces and tabletops too.

The large, solid pieces of furniture – *armoires*, cupboards, tables, chairs – are often locally made as well, usually from walnut or, less often, fruitwood, or they may be constructed from a cheaper wood which has then been painted. The chairs often have rush or cane seats.

Other robust natural textures are equally familiar in the Provencal kitchen. The floors may be covered with willow mats, while woven baskets and chunky terracotta casseroles of all shapes and sizes add further rich texture. Contrasting with all this are the cool, hard surfaces of French enamelware, wine in a wire rack and, of course, the all-important *batterie de cuisine*.

You may not have the thick stone or clay walls or the shuttered windows of the typical Provencal *mas* (farmhouse), but there's no reason why you cannot introduce some of the other elements. Paint effects like the ones covered in this chapter make an excellent starting point. Add some Provencal print curtains, table linen and cushions, suitably rustic furniture and cupboards, perhaps an *armoire* or *banquette*, and some colourful Provencal pottery, and all you'll need then is the mistral.

Although an armoire traditionally has three panels with curving edges on each of the two doors, this simpler cupboard functions in the same way. Antiquing techniques add to the impression of venerable age in furniture like this.

A soft ochre colourwash on the walls of this kitchen provides a flavour of the sun-baked South of France.

Flagstone Floor

Provencal kitchens generally have flagstone or tiled floors, but if your floor is concrete instead, you can still create the gentle colours and well-worn, aged look of flagstones. Although *trompe l'oeil* flagstones look three-dimensional, the entire effect is created with paint on a flat surface. The colours can be varied to represent limestone, sandstone or whatever type of stone is desired. The same techniques can also be used to simulate a stone wall.

1 Cover the entire floor surface with a Portland Grey vinyl silk emulsion (latex velvet) paint. At least two coats are advisable.

2 Mark out with a pencil, ruler and straightedge the pattern of the flagstones on the floor. Make the pencil marks quite light so that they can be easily erased should you need to alter the pattern. Draw the stones to what you feel is a reasonable size for a flagstone and for your floor area, or work to a size that you have measured on a real flagstone.

3 Make up a water-based glaze, adding White and a little Raw Umber to create a light brown colour. Choose one flagstone to start with and paint it very loosely with this glaze, using a brush.

4 Make up a second, darker glaze in which there is very little or no White. Paint on the second glaze in different places so that the stone is darker at one edge, lighter at another, and darker or lighter in the centre. Ensure that when you have finished one stone and are moving on to its neighbour, there is a change in tone. If it is dark on one side of the pencil line, then make it light on the other. Do this with the brush while you are applying the glaze, or with a cloth in the next step.

5 Pounce the surface with a loosely rolled-up cloth to obtain a stippled effect. Aim to have some areas lighter and others darker, all the time trying to maintain the variation on either side of the pencil line. Also ensure that the centres of neighbouring stones are different tones to make it look like all the stones are different. As you move around the floor area filling in the squares, remember to stand back and take an overall look to make sure that what you are doing resembles a series of separate flagstones. It may be a help to keep a photograph of a flagstone floor handy for reference. You can vary the material that you use to pounce the surface. Hessian (burlap), a vaiety of rags, a sponge, etc, can all be brought into service to help re-create the variable texture of stone.

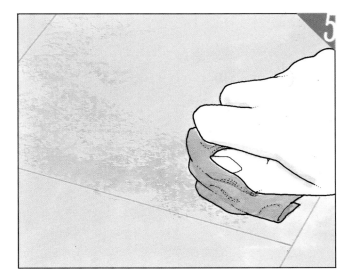

Materials Checklist

- ✸ 7.5cm (3in) decorator's brush
- ✸ Small pointed brush
- ✸ Vinyl silk emulsion (latex velvet) paint in Portland Grey
- ✸ Water-based glaze
- ✸ Acrylic paints in White and Raw Umber
- ✸ Oil crayons in Dark Raw Umber, White and Grey
- ✸ White spirit (mineral spirits) and/or oil glaze
- ✸ Polyurethane varnish

6 Once the glazes have dried, you can create the cement grouting lines where the *faux* stones join together. Take a Dark Raw Umber oil crayon and mark along all the horizontal and vertical pencil lines. Don't use a ruler, as the slight irregularities which occur when you draw freehand will help to emphasize the rough edges of the stones.

7 Work out from which direction the light (real or imaginary) will be falling on the floor. Using a White oil crayon, trace a very thin highlight along the edge of each brown line farthest from the light source, drawing it in freehand, too. This will represent the light hitting the leading edges of the flagstones, creating highlights.

8 You may also apply highlights to the brown lines running at right angles to your original highlighted lines, depending on how you feel the light source will work in the room. Wherever the leading edge of a flagstone might catch the light, a highlight should be traced in with the White oil crayon.

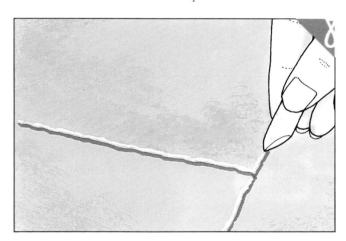

9 Study the overall effect of the areas of light and shade – you may decide that some of the white lines can be made broader and stronger, while others may need to be rubbed away altogether. Sometimes the darker lines, too, will benefit from being made slightly thicker. Real

flagstones are not perfect and there will always be variations in the gaps between them. This is another instance where a photograph will help you.

10 Simulated cracks and fissures can now be added to some of the stones. Take the dark oil crayon and draw a little jagged loop. Fill in with rubbings of a grey crayon, then gently flatten this out with a little white spirit (mineral spirits) and/or oil glaze, and a tiny brush. Now draw a very fine highlight on the outside edge of the loop away from the light source. This represents a chip which has fallen out of the stone, the dark band on one side being the shadow where the light is hitting it and the fine white line being the highlight where the light is reflected off the other edge. To simulate a fissure, apply a jagged line with the darker crayon, drawing a thin white edge along the line on the side away from the light. The number of chips, fissures or cracks you apply will depend on how old and battered you want the floor to look.

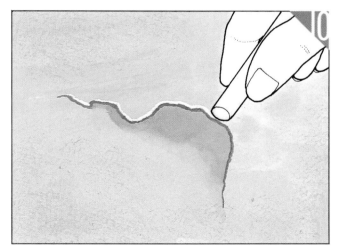

11 Finish by giving the floor at least three coats of varnish, sanding down between coats (see page 12). The varnish is essential, because the floor will obviously get a lot of wear. Also, the floor in a kitchen has to be impervious to water.

Colourwashed Walls

This project simulates the walls of an old kitchen in the South of France. The worn walls would have a terracotta paint (or other suitably earthy shade) on them aged by years of wear-and-tear and sunshine. To achieve this effect with a modern wall, you first roughen it up with all-purpose filler (spackle) and then colourwash it. To obtain the look of an aged wall, it is always better to work in two stages as described rather than to go for a darker glaze with the first coat. You have more control over depth of colour and areas of light and shade if you use two coats of glaze.

1 To make the wall look old, mix up a tub of filler and try to lay this on the wall as if you were plastering it. As plastering is a difficult skill to master, the more filler or plaster you try to apply, the more the wall will resemble a genuine, rough-plastered old wall! Or if you prefer, use repair plaster, which is suitable for amateurs. Buy it ready-mixed or as powder which is mixed with water, then apply with a plastering tool known as a float. While the plaster is still wet, rough up the surface, adjusting the angle of the float to create either a smoother or coarser effect. Change direction to create a random, choppy pattern, and rough up the plaster using the side of the float.

2 Paint your ancient wall with at least two coats of vinyl silk emulsion (latex velvet) in White, which will serve as an undercoat for the glaze.

3 Make up a water-based glaze. There is a very beautiful colour called Red Oxide which, if added to the glaze with a little Burnt Sienna, will create the lovely terracotta colour used here. Brush this glaze loosely onto the wall in patches roughly a metre (a yard) square then, using a dusting brush, stipple it out to create uneven patches – some darker and some lighter.

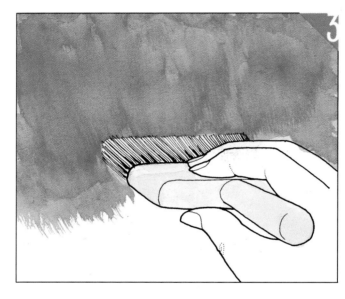

4 As the glaze begins to dry a little, soften it in all directions with a hog's hair softening brush and you will find that you have a dappled terracotta glaze with virtually no brush marks. Work rapidly, moving from area to area to ensure that you keep a wet edge going all the time (in other words, that you do not allow the edges to dry out).

5 Once the glaze has dried, repeat the process using the same glaze. This ensures that, if there are any areas which still look too white, you can compensate with the second layer of glaze. Apply very little of the second coat of glaze to areas which already look dark enough.

Materials Checklist

❁ 7.5cm (3in) decorator's brush
❁ 7.5cm (3in) dusting brush
❁ 7.5cm (3in) hog's hair softener
❁ All-purpose filler (spackle), or repair plaster and float
❁ Vinyl silk emulsion (latex velvet) in White
❁ Water-based glaze
❁ Acrylic paints in Red Oxide and Burnt Sienna

Verdigris Basket

Verdigris, the wonderful greenish blue patina found on old copper, brass and bronze, is the result of atmospheric action upon the metal surface. The ancient Greeks discovered it, and its name in fact comes from *vert de Grèce*, which means "green of Greece". It can be seen on historic domes and spires, on Greek and Roman artifacts – and on old copper piping where moist air has come into contact with the pipe to produce a turquoise blue colour.

Items with a genuine verdigris patina of age are obviously valuable, but it is not difficult to simulate the effect. In this project, a rusty old metal basket was painted and filled with flowers, and is now well suited to adorn either a rustic kitchen or a patio. Although the basket in this project is metal, a verdigris effect can also be given to non-metallic surfaces such as plaster, ceramic and even plastic. Candlesticks, lamp bases, picture frames, garden furniture and urns all lend themselves to the verdigris treatment.

Be careful when applying the rotten-stone powder used for verdigris. Always wear a mask as you must avoid breathing it in.

1 To prepare the metal basket, rub off any areas of rust with steel wool and remove any grease by washing in soapy water. To prepare a non-metallic surface, paint it first with dark brown emulsion (latex) paint.

2 Once the basket has been cleaned and dried thoroughly, apply a little goldsize and then once tack point has been reached, smooth transfer copper leaf onto several different areas, as directed for the Gilded Frames, page 51.

3 Make up a mix of turquoise blue by taking White and adding to it some of the Viridian Green and Cerulean Blue, dirtying this up ever so slightly with the smallest amount of Raw Umber. Tap this on all over the metal, tapping it loosely and leaving plenty of bare areas, especially where there is copper leaf.

4 Make up a lighter version of the turquoise using more White and a darker version using more Raw Umber. Tap on both to fill some of the bare areas, remembering to leave plenty of little bits of copper showing through.

5 Blend all of the above by tapping with a brush then tap the rotten-stone powder into various areas of the metal basket. This creates the aged look and also the rough texture seen in the real metal.

6 Using a fitch brush, gently touch in some areas of the basket with Raw Sienna to give a slightly yellow tinge to the bluish colour.

7 Use a light mix of the turquoise colour to tap in some highlights, adapting the final appearance to suit your personal taste. Finish with one or two coats of varnish if you plan to use it for plants that will need watering.

The Cottage Style Bedroom

C OSY AND SMALL-SCALE, cottage style decor is easy
to live with. Nothing is grand or ornate. Simple
furnishings and natural materials predominate:
cotton fabrics, pine furniture, rush matting. Similarly,
highly finished paint effects like marbling would look
completely alien in a cottage style interior.

The beauty of paint effects for cottage style
bedrooms is that simplicity, rather than elaborate or
difficult effects, works best. The bedroom on the right,
for example, looks lovely with plain wide painted
stripes in soft tones of blue and yellow. (For how to
paint stripes, see pages 112-13.)

Painted stripes are used in a different way on page 90.
By using them to form panels, in tones of pink, they
frame the pretty four-poster bed rather than clashing
with it. Notice how the bands are painted with shadows
along the top and lefthand edges, and highlights along
the bottom and righthand edges, to create a simple three-
dimensional effect. (A similar technique is used in the
project on pages 70-1.) Stencilling here and there
completes the wall decoration in this room.

In the photograph below, not only is paint utilized to call attention to the bedhead, but it actually *is* the headboard. This *trompe l'oeil* headboard has a charming rustic quality about it that is perfect for cottage style decor. To create a similar effect yourself, draw in the outline, then paint in the basic colour. Now paint a rim of shadow around it to imitate the shadow that a real headboard would cast. The flowers can be stencilled, or painted in by tracing then hand-colouring.

The flowers, leaves and stems in the room on page 92 (top) are also painted in by hand after tracing the design on the wall. Sometimes understatement has the most impact; here the delicate flowers and soft colours echo the soft grey beams and gentle yellow walls.

PRECEDING SPREAD: In a cottage style bedroom, simple paint effects like these stripes work best.

OPPOSITE: Toning panels of colour, with basic shading and highlighting, are arranged to frame the furniture and echo the rectangular shapes in this cottage bedroom.

LEFT: At first glance this appears to be a prettily painted headboard, but it is in fact a painted picture of a headboard.

TOP: As with much stencilling, the appeal of this hand-painting lies in its muted, faded look.

BOTTOM: Cottages tend to have small rooms with low ceilings and awkward angles, and a soft colourwash on walls and ceiling is an effective way of unifying the room.

The soft, parchment-like paint finish on the walls and ceiling shown below help to unify and disguise the awkward angles of the room. The colourwash is created in the usual way, by rubbing a glaze over the wall leaving cloudy patches. The cupboard, painted in the grey emulsion (latex) or distemper (calcimine) used for all the woodwork, has had some of the glaze rubbed onto it, creating a timeworn look.

A very different type of camouflage is used on page 93. It is achieved by covering the walls and cupboard doors with a wallpaper or fabric, then sticking similar pictures such as flower prints in an orderly way on the doors. Stick on a trim such as narrow braid to frame them individually. The idea can be extended even further, so that you can use colour photocopies of Victorian prints, edge-to-edge to completely cover a wall or portion of a wall.

Floor-to-ceiling prints stuck to fabric- or paper-covered doors and walls will make the area look less bitty and therefore more spacious.

Wood-Grained Chest

This chest began life as an inexpensive self-assembly chest made from MDF (medium density fibreboard). Some simple wood-graining has transformed it into a handsome piece of furniture seemingly made from bird's eye maple.

Bird's eye maple is a wood often found in cottages, particularly on the walls in the form of picture frames. From the eighteenth to the mid nineteenth century, it was one of the most widely imitated woods. Although relatively large areas, such as panelling, were grained to look like bird's eye maple, the effect is also very well suited to picture frames and boxes – and, of course, the chest-of-drawers of this project.

Top-class decorators in Victorian times were able to simulate a variety of woods including maple, oak, mahogany and walnut. They used techniques which survive to this day, although they are now far less commonplace. In a house where cheap wood like pine was used – for example, on skirtings (baseboards), doors or cornices (crown moldings) – the Victorian craftsman would grain the wood to look like more expensive timber. Part of a room might even have been clad or panelled with beautiful mahogany, but where the mahogany ran out, cheaper panelling would be installed and grained to match the mahogany.

Today wood graining is appreciated as much for its craftsmanship as for its economical value. As well as the financial saving, the use of the wood-graining technique is ecologically valuable, because treating a cheap material to make it look like an expensive wood helps save the endangered rain forests. For example, the compact wood chipboard used here can be painted to look like virtually any type of wood.

Materials Checklist

✪ *Decorator's brush*
✪ *Wavy mottler*
✪ *Badger softener*
✪ *Eggshell paint in a honey or cinnamon colour*
✪ *Scouring pad*
✪ *Vinegar*
✪ *Powder colour in Burnt Umber*
✪ *Pencil with rubber (eraser)*
✪ *Distemper (calcimine) paint in a bluish black shade (optional)*
✪ *Varnish*
✪ *Wax*

1 Give the chest of drawers two coats of a honey- or cinnamon-coloured eggshell paint. This is the base colour to replicate the bird's eye maple that was popular during the Art Deco period of the 1930s.

2 You will be using a water-based glaze on the eggshell surface, but water will not wet the oil-based eggshell very well. Traditionally, this problem was solved by rubbing the surface with a chalk called whiting. An easier, modern method is to rub the surface with a green scouring pad, which will allow the water-based glaze to lie evenly all over.

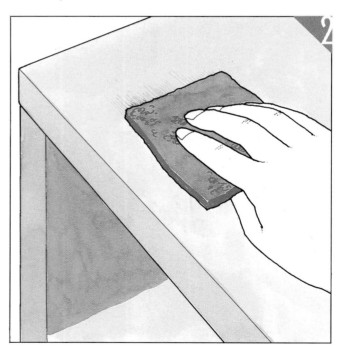

3 Mix up equal parts of water and vinegar. Apply a coat of this glaze all over the surface.

4 The first specialist brush used in this process is called a wavy mottler. Barely touch the vinegar-and-water mixture with the wavy mottler, and then dab it lightly into the Burnt Umber powder. Now rub it all over the surface until you have a fairly even light brown colour.

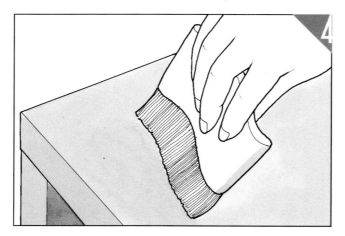

5 Again using the mottler, press gently down onto the surface with your fingers in the bristles, then lift off. This will leave a clear spot in the glaze. Repeat this process, moving rapidly across the surface pressing down and lifting off until you have created a series of light and dark patches. For it to look right, you need to be able to do this quickly, both across the surface and then down the surface. Practise on a small area first, but once you have mastered the technique, you will be able to move your wrist or fingers in rippling movements to vary the effect and stop the pattern from looking too rigid.

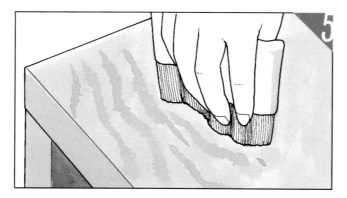

6 The next stage should also be practised in a small area. It involves the use of a badger softening brush, which is the only brush which can be used to soften a water-based substance, as the badger hair will completely shed the water. Soften from side to side over the marks you have made with the mottler, to remove some of the moisture. Now soften up and down to spread the dark bands very slightly.

7 Once you find you can accomplish this in a small area, move on to larger areas. On a project the size of this chest you should be able to complete the drawer fronts fairly quickly, but you may need more practice for the top and the sides. The key is to move quickly and if you ever decide to use this method for larger projects – a wardrobe door, for example – then you will need to work with an assistant. As you ripple the top with the mottler, your assistant works below you brushing on the Burnt Umber glaze to make sure it is still wet when you come to it. It is possible to cover large areas such as doors, staircase handrails and columns in this way.

8 Bird's eye maple, of course, takes its name from the so-called eyes in the wood. These are little bumps surrounded by a ring. There are all sorts of eyes in the real wood, from lone rings or parts of rings to dots only partially enclosed by the ring, or dots sitting completely alone. The wood may also have a dense covering of eyes, or it may only have a few single eyes spaced out in an area or perhaps small clusters. One quick way to create these eyes is to use a rubber- (eraser-) tipped pencil. Cut out the centre of the rubber tip with the point of a craft knife or scalpel (mat knife) to create a ring and then tap this into the darker bits of the wet mottling. You can create a variety of rings in this way and then tap the edge of the rubber tip in the centre of the ring to make the dot in the middle.

9 An even simpler method is to simply press your knuckle into the darker bits of the mottling. This is the method that was used here. Soften the eyes gently with the badger brush so that they don't stand out so strongly. You will then have an almost perfect simulation of bird's eye maple.

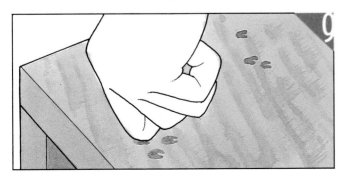

10 In this chest the drawer handles and the feet have been painted with a bluish black distemper (calcimine) paint. This adds an important element of variety to an item which is completely covered by a single paint effect.

11 Once the surface is dry, apply three coats of varnish, sanding between coats (see page 12). Rub the last coat with wax.

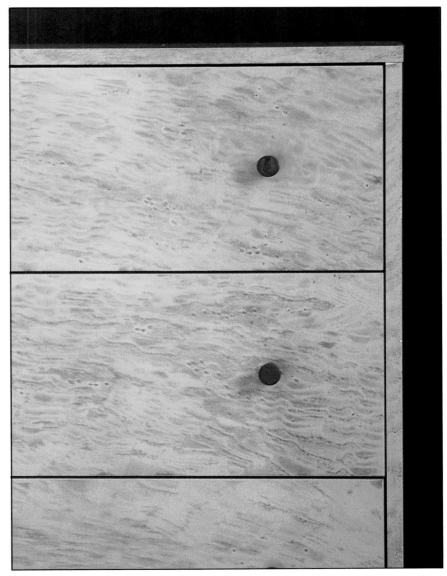

Covered Hat Boxes

Hat boxes covered with paper look chic and are also very functional, particularly in a cottage bedroom where there may not be a great deal of storage space. Use odds and ends of wallpaper to match your decor, and/or a coordinating wallpaper border – or perhaps an expensive hand-made paper, since you don't actually need very much. Trimming the box with a contrasting paper gives it a smart, professional-looking finish.

1 Measure the distance around the box and the depth. On the wrong side of the paper, draw a rectangle to these dimensions plus 1.2cm (1/2in) extra on each edge. This strip will wrap around the sides of the box, so be sure to take into account the direction of stripes or other pattern when positioning the rectangle. Cut out the paper strip.

2 Apply glue to the back side of the strip and stick the strip around the sides of the box so that the same amount of paper projects beyond each edge. Overlap the ends of the strip. Using a slightly damp sponge, wipe from the centre out to the edges to press out any creases or air bubbles.

3 Snip into the extra paper around both edges at regular intervals. Reapply glue to the edges if necessary, and turn the paper to the inside along the top of the box, and onto the base along the other edge. Make sure it is securely glued in place.

4 Draw around the base of the box onto the paper, and cut out. Glue this circle onto the base to cover the snipped edges.

5 Draw around the lid onto the wrong side of the paper, then draw another circle around it, making the new circle 1.2cm (1/2in) bigger all around. Snip around the edge at regular intervals, stopping just short of the inner circle. Glue the circle to the top of the lid, sticking the snipped edges all around the rim.

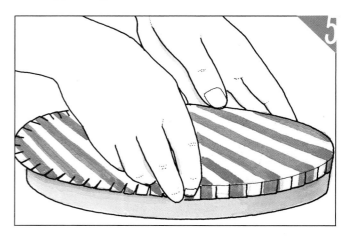

6 Cut a strip of paper as wide as the depth of the lid, and as long as the distance around it plus 1.2cm (1/2in). Glue this around the rim of the lid, overlapping the ends.

7 If desired, use an eyelet tool to make two holes in the box, on opposite sides, just below the lid, then insert the ends of a length of ribbon or cord through them. Knot on the inside.

8 Either leave the box plain, or decorate the lid with trimmings of your choice, such as buttons, eyelets, ribbon or lace edging. Alternatively, glue cut-out pictures or silhouettes onto the sides or lid.

Materials Checklist
✿ *Round hat box*
✿ *Paper*
✿ *PVA glue (white glue)*
✿ *Eyelet tool (optional)*
✿ *Ribbon or cord (optional)*
✿ *Buttons, lace edging, ribbon or other trim (optional)*

Découpage Screen

The technique of découpage can be used to decorate all manner of surfaces, from flat boxes, trays and table mats to tins, watering cans and wastebaskets, and even wardrobes, bedheads, trunks and screens.

The images you can use are equally varied. Colour photocopies of old maps or botanical prints, flowers cut from wrapping paper, greetings cards, old calendars, seed packets or catalogues – the list is endless.

The découpage technique is simplicity itself and involves cutting out paper pictures, gluing them onto the surface and then varnishing repeatedly. This last stage is important, as it not only protects the cut-outs but it makes them look like painted decoration, which is the whole point of the technique.

Traditionally, up to 100 coats of varnish were used and lightly sanded after the first 20 or so coats, but today 20 coats in total is more usual. Or, if you do not mind a finish that is not so smooth, you could use only six or seven coats.

Materials Checklist
✿ *Paper designs of flowers or other images*
✿ *Print sealer or PVA diluted with water (1 part PVA to 2 parts water)*
✿ *Emulsion (latex) paint in cream (optional)*
✿ *PVA glue (white glue)*
✿ *Matt (flat) polyurethane varnish*
✿ *Very fine steel wool*

1 Before cutting out, you should ideally coat both sides of the design sparingly with sealer, to prevent the varnish affecting it. Now, using a scalpel (mat knife) and cutting board, or sharp, pointed scissors, cut out the designs, carefully cutting away all the background around the images.

2 Sand the surface and wipe it to remove any grease or dust. Either seal it too or apply a couple of coats of emulsion (latex) paint, allowing it to dry between coats.

3 Plan the arrangement of the images, then glue them to the surface. Using a cloth or sponge, smooth them

down from the centre outwards, being careful to stick down the edges completely. Wipe away any surplus glue. Leave to dry.

4 Paint on thin coats of varnish, allowing it to dry between coats. After about 12 coats, lightly sand with the steel wool, then add two more coats. Sand lightly again. Repeat as many times as necessary until the designs look as though they are painted on, finishing with the varnish.

The Modern Style Bedroom for Kids

PAINT EFFECTS ARE GREAT FUN in children's rooms because you can relax and let your – or your child's – imagination run riot. Bright, cheerful primary colours somehow seem right in a child's room, so why not be really bold and use them in exciting patterns and shapes? In the photograph on the right, deliberately patchy, uneven stripes in red, yellow and blue match the bedcover and pillowcase. (For various ways to paint stripes, see pages 112-13.)

Colourful spots are an alternative to stripes. Choose a coordinating paper and border, such as the blue with yellow spots on page 104, then choose a contrasting colour like pink. This is a triadic colour scheme – using three colours that are equally spaced on the colour wheel. So is the scheme on the right, and in fact, they both use the same colours, only this one uses tints

PRECEDING SPREAD: Children's rooms provide a good opportunity to be adventurous with colours and patterns.

RIGHT: This room knocks spots off more timid uses of pattern and colour. Even the doorknob looks like a polkadot.

OPPOSITE: A modern decor offers scope for strong contrasts and abstract patterns, both of which work well in children's rooms.

(pastels) rather than the fully saturated hues. Although the whole point of a lively, bold use of colour is the freedom to break the rules, you will probably find that contrasting schemes like this work best when the colours are not used in equal amounts.

The pink is used not only on the skirting (baseboard) and dado rail (chair rail) but also on the door panels, which are sponged yellow with pink spots, and on the doorknob. The bright yellow above the border is also in the colour scheme, and the soft

furnishings coordinate with the wallpaper border. In fact, wallpaper borders are remarkably versatile. Use one above a dado rail, or actually to create a dado rail (a useful trick if your ceilings seem too high). Alternatively, instead of putting it on the wall, run one around a piece of furniture such as a toy box, or use it on the panels of a door. Another idea is to cut out images from a border – particularly if you have used the same border elsewhere in the room – and découpage these (see page 100) onto some sort of surface.

For a bright, cheerful look that is dramatic too, combine strong primary colours and abstract shapes against a white background, as in the room on page 105.

For a very different look, try sticking newspapers or comics on one wall, as in the room shown above, all in an orderly grid arrangement. To make the surface practical, however, you will need to varnish it.

There's always a place for the small and sweet cuddly animal in a young child's room. When a child has dozens of soft toys, the animals can climb the walls instead! For example, the stencilled rabbits hopping around the room on page 106 would delight any young child.

An unused fireplace offers much potential for fun, imaginative paintwork. The decorative painting in the picture on page 108 has transformed the fireplace – which had already been turned into a useful cupboard, with a door and shelf – into a Moorish castle. This is a good example of how you can allow restrictions to inspire rather than inhibit you – the cardinal rule when using paint and paper in a child's room.

Sponged Table

Pieces of junk furniture make an excellent basis for paint effects that will transform them into attractively mellow-looking furniture. The old discarded table used here, which was in fairly poor condition, has been given a new lease of life with simple sponged decoration. Distemper (calcimine) glazes were used, for a soft, chalky effect. Not only is the table now ideal for a child's room but it would also look good elsewhere in the house.

The decoration used here is quite simple but you may prefer a more elaborate design, depending on the shape of the table. Try sketching potential designs on the table top. Also, as distemper paints dry so quickly, you can even paint in rough versions of the designs to help you decide what will look best. Here, the table top was divided into segments running into a circular motif consisting of concentric rings at the centre of the table.

The segments are painted in alternating colours. Each segment is isolated with masking tape running from the edge to the centre of the table top. The colour can then be simply sponged on.

The colours used here are glazes made up from distemper to which a little water-based glaze is added. A rusty red and a green were used in this instance, but you can choose colours to suit your interior decor.

1 Begin by painting the entire table – top and bottom – in white distemper (calcimine) to seal the wood and give a good base for the next stage. Paint the base of the table with straw yellow distemper.

2 Lightly pencil in your design, drawing around different-sized round objects such as glasses for the central circles.

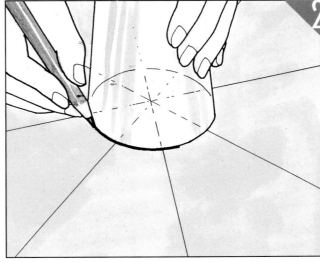

Hint

A hair dryer can be used to help speed up the paint-drying process.

3 Run strips of masking tape along both edges of one segment; there is no need to mask the circular motif at the centre.

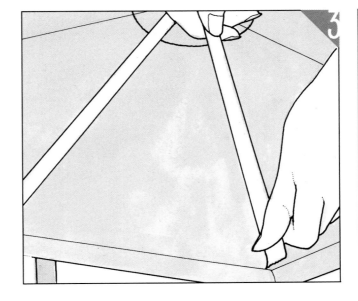

Materials Checklist

- ✪ *Decorator's brush*
- ✪ *Fine artist's brush*
- ✪ *Good-quality marine sponge*
- ✪ *Distemper (calcimine) paints in white, straw yellow, rusty red and green shades*
- ✪ *Water-based glaze*
- ✪ *Varnish (optional)*

4 Mix up a glaze of distemper in your first colour, diluted with a little water-based glaze. Sponge on the glaze between the lengths of tape. To sponge on (as opposed to sponging off, which involves removing glaze with a sponge to create a textured effect), dampen your sponge a little with water, then take up some of the glaze onto the sponge. The amount of glaze you pick up is important – too little and it will just look speckly, too much and it will look muddy – so test it first on a piece of cardboard. Sponge on haphazardly over the whole segment, then go back and fill in until you have the degree of coverage you want.

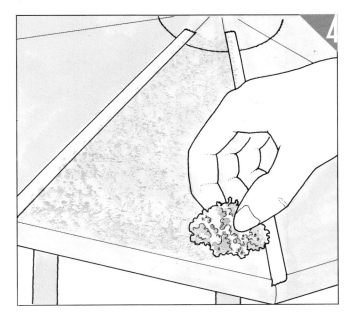

5 Repeat the procedure for the other segments in the same colour. Leave to dry then remove the masking tape. Repeat for the remaining segments, using the other colour, so the tabletop is covered with alternating colours. Finally, using a paintbrush, paint in the circular motif at the centre in one or both colours.

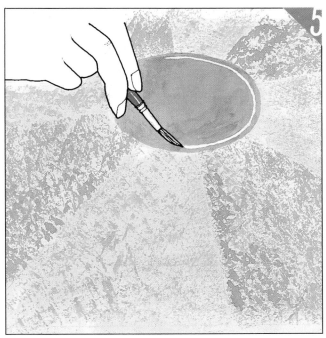

6 If the table is likely to receive much use – as it certainly will in a child's room – it is advisable to varnish it (see page 12).

Painted Stripes

Painted stripes are fun and colourful in a child's room and can be used in a variety of imaginative ways. Here they form a painted dado, reaching up to a horizontal stripe at dado rail (chair rail) height. The colour used for the mock dado rail is also used for the stencilled diamond border at the top of the wall.

The stripes can be all the same width or varying widths, and in just one or two colours or in multi-colours. Note that the paint you use will need to be fairly thick.

1 For stripes with sharp, straight edges like those shown here, use a plumb line and spirit level to draw vertical and horizontal lines. Mask the edges with low-tack masking tape, then apply the paint with a brush.

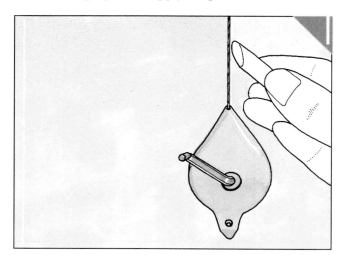

Materials Checklist

✺ Decorator's
brush and/or
roller
✺ Emulsion
(latex) paint

2 For a less precise effect, do not mask the edges. Paint the stripes using a roller that is the desired width – perhaps 23cm (9in) or 15cm (6in) or even 2.5cm (3in). Follow a plumb line for the first stripe to keep it

straight, then use a piece of cardboard as a spacing guide for subsequent stripes. If you want a textured finish, simply run the roller down the wall without going over the surface more than once (except to fill in any really uneven patches). You can paint the stripes over a background colour, using it as one of the stripe colours, or apply two alternating colours over a base coat, with the edges overlapping slightly. Because the roller cannot get right up to a dado rail or skirting (baseboard), you will need to finish off with a brush the same width as the stripes.

3 For an even livelier look, paint the stripes freehand, without masking tape, using a decorator's brush the width of the stripe or a sponge. Wobbly lines are deliberate here!

4 For squiggly stripes, tie string tightly around a foam paint roller at the centre and at both ends, then use this to paint the roller stripes. Run it down the wall in one continuous movement.

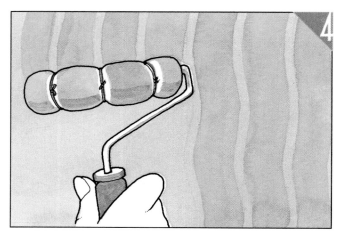

Stencilled Star Borders

Stencilling is another paint effect which is so versatile that it can be adapted to any room and any style of decor. Here a simple star stencil is used around the tops of the walls and, in the reversed colourway, on a painted border at dado rail (chair rail) height.

1 Paint a horizontal border using a spirit level (carpenter's level) and low-tack masking tape to make it level and the edges sharp.

2 Make a star template and use it to draw a line of evenly spaced stars on stencil card (or acetate, but this is harder to cut), leaving a reasonable margin between the motifs and the edge of the card. The top margin should be the desired distance of the border from the cornice (crown molding) or ceiling. (Alternatively, if you leave a larger margin at the top you will be able to fold the stencil so that the fold fits into the angle between wall and ceiling, and the margin beyond it protects the ceiling from paint.)

3 Place the stencil card on thick cardboard or a cutting mat, and use a craft knife or scalpel (mat knife) to carefully cut out the stars. Hold the knife almost straight up and down, and cut towards you, with your free hand steadying the card behind the knife. To change direction, turn the stencil rather than the knife. Make sure that your knife or scalpel is sharp; a dull blade is dangerous.

4 Use low-tack masking tape to tape the stencil in place either along the top of the wall or along the centre of the border.

5 Put some paint into a paint tray or onto a paper plate. Take up some colour on your brush or sponge and then dab it onto some absorbent paper (paper towel) or the paper plate – you should always take great care to avoid having much paint on it.

6 Hold the brush (if using) at right angles to the surface, with your free hand holding the stencil in place. Use the brush or sponge to apply the paint with a gentle stippling, or pouncing, motion, making short up-and-down jabbing movements from above. This is one traditional stencilling technique, but an alternative method involves making light circular movements. Try both effects, and decide which you prefer.

7 Once you have stencilled all the stars on the stencil, untape and lift it straight away from the wall. Remove any paint from the back and then reposition it, with the end star on the stencil over the last star just completed. Continue stencilling in the same way. Varnish the surface to protect it from young fingers.

Materials Checklist

❂ *Decorator's brush*
❂ *Stencil brush or small sponge*
❂ *Stencil card or acetate*
❂ *Craft knife or scalpel (mat knife)*
❂ *Emulsion (latex) paints*

The Colonial Style Bathroom

AMERICA'S COLONIAL PERIOD extended from the first settlements at the beginning of the seventeenth century until the American Revolution in 1776, when the Federal style developed. There were, of course, no bathrooms in the colonists' houses, but the style lends itself very well to this room nevertheless.

The key to understanding colonial style is to remember the colonists' circumstances. Coming from all over Europe, they had brought styles and techniques of their mother countries with them to the New World, yet were unable to bring many actual material items. In trying to make their homes comfortable and attractive, they attempted to recreate the homes they had left behind – but using the materials of the new continent. In particular, they attempted to simulate the expensive, rare woods like mahogany and walnut which were no longer available to them.

Gradually the very diverse traditions began to converge, and America's homes, like its folk art,

developed their own unique style and national identity. One factor in this was the itinerant decorators who travelled the countryside, decorating people's homes in return for food and lodging, and using much the same style wherever they went.

The paints that were used were made from vegetable pigments mixed with strained stale buttermilk. Oil paints made from vegetable pigments and minerals mixed with linseed oil were also available.

Stencilling and various forms of wood graining were particularly popular. In comparison with today's finely detailed, highly finished work, colonial paintwork was quite crude. However, like folk art, the naive style, strong contrasts and dense areas of colour look very appealing in an appropriate context.

Today the term Shaker is often used to mean colonial. The Shakers were a religious sect founded in the late eighteenth century. Their numbers were greatest in the early nineteenth century, but after that they steadily dwindled. Famous throughout the world for their simple, uncluttered designs and superb craftsmanship, they believed in applying order, harmony, utility, self-discipline and a search for excellence to every aspect of their lives. This meant stripping away all superfluous ornamentation from their homes, yet at the same time making sure that every detail was as good as it could be.

Authentic re-creations of Shaker rooms can be seen today, and the style is instantly recognizable. A sense of tranquillity and harmony pervades the atmosphere. In the light, airy and spotlessly clean rooms, the sash (double-hung) windows are bare, as are the polished floorboards, and the walls are whitewashed. Beautiful built-in wooden cupboards line some of the walls, and many walls have pegboards from which are neatly hung all manner of things, from ladderback chairs to brooms. Other than that, the walls are bare too.

With their dislike of sham, the Shakers refused to use veneers or the wood graining that were popular

among "the world's people", as they called the outside world. They also avoided stencilling since that was regarded as unnecessary decoration.

What they did do, however, was paint or stain much of the woodwork, including dado rails (chair rails), skirting boards (baseboards) and window and door frames, in lovely rich colours. This served a practical purpose, in protecting the wood, so it was allowed. From the 1830s, two solid colours, or one solid colour with natural wood, were often combined. They also painted or stained their distinctive oval storage boxes in order to colour-code the contents, and these are, of course, highly popular today.

The colour most associated with the Shakers is the deep blue-green used in the bathroom on pages 116-17. In fact, this colour was made from the most expensive pigment and so was reserved for their meeting-houses, where they met to worship. Colours they did use in their homes included sage green, yellow ochre, red ochre, cranberry and brown.

The bathroom in the photograph on pages 116-17 actually avoids the multitude of ornaments that are today erroneously described as Shaker. Functional and uncluttered, it has all the characteristic elements, including a pegboard, built-in cupboards, wood floors, white walls and meeting-house blue painted woodwork.

The bathroom on page 119 is obviously not Shaker, but it does have a colonial feeling about it. The bright blue painted Lincrusta wallpaper makes an attractive alternative to tiles and goes well with the claw-foot bath, natural wood and checked floor.

A colonial style bathroom does not have to have plain painted walls. In fact, even a sprigged wallpaper (vinyl or vinyl-coated for the bathroom) would look right in colonial style, though not, obviously, in Shaker style. On page 120, striped green and yellow wallpaper is used on the dado, with the green matched in the paintwork of the bath. White walls above the dado, and white woodwork, keep the effect crisp.

Antiqued Wood

Antiqued, distressed wood is very much at home in today's interiors, nowhere more so than in a colonial-style room. In the bathroom, antiqued tongue-and-groove panelling makes a plain, unfussy and cosy alternative to tiles. It will make the bathroom look time-worn, lived-in and interesting rather than clinical.

Distemper (calcimine) paint was used here for its soft, chalky effect, but you could use emulsion (latex) paint instead. Similarly, for the two layers of paint, you could use different colours than the greenish blue and green in the photograph. Tones that are similar will look soft and mellow, while contrasting colours can look dramatic. Generally, the darker colour should go underneath.

1 Using a cloth, wipe over the woodwork with a dark pine wood-stain. This will leave the wood looking like dark pine, even though the wood you are working on is basically a much newer and cheaper, rapidly grown modern timber.

2 Paint the woodwork with a dark bluish green distemper (calcimine) paint, brushing it on all over. When it is dry, rub it back in places, using wet-and-dry paper with soapy water, in order to allow patches of the dark wood to show through. These patches will represent worn areas. Some of the worn areas should be chosen simply because they look pleasing to the eye, perhaps in the middle of the door or on one or two of the planks on the wall. Other areas will simulate wear-and-tear, such as the edge and top of the door frame, parts of the chair rail, as well as the leading edge of the door and the area around the door knob, both of which are continually rubbed by people's hands.

3 Now rub these open wood areas with a candle. The greasy wax will keep them clear of any paint that is applied subsequently, so it will look as though the paint has worn away over the years in these areas.

4 Painting a crackleglaze medium on top of a water-based paint (such as distemper), and then covering it with another coat of water-based paint, will produce cracks in the paint, simulating areas of paintwork exposed to years of sunshine. Select a few areas where you feel the crazed paint effect might be appropriate and apply the crackleglaze medium thickly. Allow it to dry thoroughly.

Materials Checklist

- *7.5cm (3in) decorator's brush*
- *Wood-stain in dark pine shade*
- *Distemper (calcimine) paint in a dark bluish green, a slightly lighter dark green and a medium green*
- *Household candle*
- *Crackleglaze medium*
- *Paint-stripper (optional)*

5 Two other distemper paints – a dark green (not quite so dark as the base colour) and a medium green – should now be used. Paint the dark green over all areas except those which have been deliberately left bare. Brush it on quite freely so that some areas will have a thick layer of green and others a thin coat which allows some of the base colour to show through. Then rub the lighter green paint into the dark green in areas where you want it to look like another colour is beginning to appear due to wear-and-tear in the dark green top coat. Step back and take an overall look at your work to make sure that you are achieving the right effect.

6 Once the greens have dried completely, rub the surface with some fairly coarse sandpaper, blending the lighter green into the dark green. Don't touch the areas of bare wood or the crackled areas. As you rub, keep checking the overall effect to make sure that the balance is right.

7 If you feel that there are too many areas where the dark bluish-green is coming through, then paint on some more of the dark green. Let this dry and then blend it in with the sandpaper. You can adjust the other colours in a similar manner. The distemper paint can be force-dried with a hair dryer, which makes it easier to carry out these important corrections. You must continually evaluate the effect in order to produce an overall picture of natural wear-and-tear.

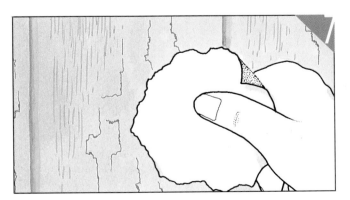

8 Tearing through paint is called distressing. You might like to carry out some rougher distressing where the paint should look chipped rather than worn. Again, choose areas where you feel this will look natural, perhaps where a chair could have hit the wall or a piece of furniture might have banged into the door frame. This sort of distressing can be done by painting on a spot or patch of paint stripper. When the paint underneath starts to bubble as the stripper bites in, take a stick with a cloth wrapped around it and hit the paint-stripped area. The underlying paint will be chipped off.

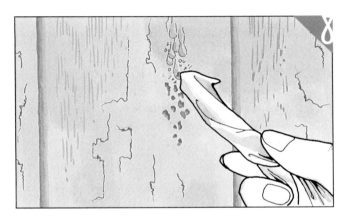

Checked Walls

Painted panelling and block-printed walls are both authentic treatments for colonial style rooms, and softly textured checks make an attractive change from modern tiles. You could use two tones that are very close to each other, as in the bathroom shown here, or one colour on a white background, depending upon how much contrast you like. If desired, the effect can be softened with a wash of diluted white emulsion (latex) painted over the checks.

Blocks can be made from a variety of materials, ranging from a lino or wood block or a rubber stamp, to a sponge or even a potato. The instructions here are for using a square synthetic sponge.

If you prefer to paint checks rather than print them, draw in a grid then use low-tack masking tape in vertical and horizontal lines to section off the squares and fill in with paint. This will produce a flatter, less textured look than a sponge.

Yet another check effect can be done by masking off squares in the same way then using a mini sponge roller to paint in the squares, which gives a very textured effect. The squares will be the same width as the roller – for example, about 7.5cm (3in) or 15cm (6in).

1 Prepare the surface and apply the base colour over the whole surface. Pour the darker emulsion (latex) into a paint tray or a flat dish. There is no need to draw lines before printing.

2 Pick up some paint on the sponge and press it onto scrap paper to check the effect. Once you are happy with the way it looks, press the loaded sponge firmly onto the painted surface.

3 Make the next square diagonally below the first one with the corners just touching. The third square should be at the same level as the first one, with the corners just touching the second square.

4 Continue in the same way, lining up corners, until the whole surface is covered. Clean the sponge as necessary so it won't become blocked with paint. Don't worry if the effect is uneven – that is part of the charm of hand printing!

5 If you want to blur the outline a little, creating a softer effect, paint over the whole surface with an emulsion wash (diluted 1:5).

6 In a bathroom (or kitchen) the surface will need to be varnished to protect it from moisture.

Materials Checklist

❁ *Emulsion (latex) paint in a background colour such as pale green and a deeper colour such as mid green*
❁ *Emulsion paint in off-white (optional)*
❁ *Square synthetic sponge*
❁ *Matt (flat) water-based varnish*

Useful Addresses

The following companies supply specialist paint/paper materials by post.

BRODIE & MIDDLETON LTD
68 Drury Lane
London WC2B 5SP
England
Tel (0171) 836-3289
(Brushes, powders, pigments, metallic powders)

CORNELISSEN & SON LTD
105 Great Russell St
London WC1B 3RY
England
Tel (0171) 636-1045
(Period-style paints, powder pigments, gilding materials and artist's quality brushes)

THE DOVER BOOKSHOP
18 Earlham St
London WC2H 9LN
England
Tel (0171) 836-2111
(Books to cut up for découpage)

FARROW & BALL
33 Uddens Trading Estate
Wimbourne
Dorset BH21 7NL
England
Tel (01202) 876141
(Manufacturers of the National Trust range of historic paint colours)

HEART OF THE COUNTRY
Home Farm
Swinfen
Nr Lichfield
Staffordshire WS14 9QR
Tel (01543) 481612
(Reproduction American colonial colours)

E MILNERS DECORATORS'
MERCHANT
Glanville Rd
Cowley, Oxford OX4 2DB
England
Tel (01865) 718171
England
(Specialist painting materials)

JOHN MYLAND LTD
80 Norwood High St
London SE27 9NW
England
Tel (0181) 670-9161
(Materials including liming wax, pigments, powder colours, rotten-stone and oil glaze, and brushes)

ORNAMENTA LTD
PO BOX 784
London SW7 2TB
England
Tel (0171) 584-3857
(*Trompe l'oeil* cut-out paper decorations and wallpaper)

PAINT MAGIC
116 Sheen Rd
Richmond
TW9 1UR
England
Tel (0181) 940-5503
(Paint effect kits, colourwash, woodwash, crackle glaze, stencilling supplies)

PAPERS & PAINTS
4 Park Walk
London SW10 OAD
England
Tel (0171) 352-8626
(Paints, including historic colours, brushes and other decorating materials and brushes)

E PLOTON (SUNDRIES) LTD
273 Archway Rd
London N6 5AA
England
Tel (0181) 348-0315
(Specialist brushes, metallic powders, stencilling and gilding materials, crackle varnish)

POTMOLEN PAINT
27 Woodcock Industrial Estate
Warminster
Wiltshire BA12 9DX
England
Tel (01985) 213960
(Traditional paints including distempers and limewashes)

J H RATCLIFFE
135a Linaker St
Southport PR8 5DF
England
Tel (01704) 537999
(Wood-graining and marbling products, glazing materials and brushes)

THE SHAKER SHOP
25 Harcourt St
London W1H 1DT
England
Tel (0171) 724-7672
(Reproduction Shaker buttermilk paints)

STUART R STEVENSON
68 Clerkenwell Rd
London EC1M 5QA
England
Tel (0171) 253-1693
(Artist's materials and pigments, gilding materials)

ART SUPPLY WAREHOUSE
360 Main Ave (Rte 7)
Norwalk. CT 06851
USA
Tel (800) 243-5038
or, in CT, (203) 846-2270
(Artists' brushes, paints and other supplies)

DOVER PUBLICATIONS
Dept 23
31 E 2nd St
Mineola, NY 11501
USA
(Reference books for découpage, period paints and stencils)

LIBERTY PAINTS
Rtes 66 and 23B
Hudson, NY 12534
USA
Tel (518) 828-4060
(Materials and tools including paints, glazes, brushes)

THE OLD-FASHIONED
MILK PAINT COMPANY
PO Box 222
436 Main St
Groton, MA 01450-0222
USA
Tel (508) 448-6336
(Milk paint, lime in powdered form, crackle glaze)

PEARL PAINT
308 Canal St
New York, NY 10013
USA
Tel (212) 221-6845
(Decorating and artists' paints, brushes, graining tools, stencilling materials, paints)

PLAID ENTERPRISES INC
PO Box 7600
Norcross, GA 30091-7600
USA
(Découpage supplies including paste, sealer, antiquings, gold leaf sizing)

POTTERY BARN
100 N Point St
San Francisco, CA 94133
USA
Tel (800) 922-5507
(metallic paints, marbling kits)

SEPP LEAF PRODUCTS
381 Park Ave South
Suite 1301
New York, NY 10016
USA
Tel (212) 683-2840
(Gold leaf supplies)

THE STULB COMPANY
PO Box 597
E Allen & N Graham Sts
Allentown, PA 18105-0597
USA
Tel (215) 433-4273
(Reproduction colonial paint colours)

WOOD FINISHING SUPPLY
COMPANY
100 Throop St
Palmyra, NY 14522
USA
Tel (315) 597-3743
(Glazes, varnishes, gold leaf, japan colours, graining combs, brushes)

Harry Levinson runs courses in all aspects of decorative painting. If you wish to learn more about the techniques covered in this book as well as many other techniques, contact him at:
HAMPSTEAD
DECORATIVE ARTS
2/20 Highgate High Street
London N6 5JG
England
Tel (0181) 348-2811

Acknowledgements

Projects carried out by Harry Levinson: pp 21-3, 24-6, 38-40, 41-3, 44-7,
51-3, 66-9, 70-1, 81-3, 84-5, 86-7, 94-7, 109-11 and 121-3.
Angel medallion on p 68 painted by Rosalind Williams.

PHOTOGRAPHIC CREDITS

The publishers wish to thank the following photographers and organizations for their
kind permission to reproduce their photographs:

Front cover: Abode/Trevor Richards
Back cover: David Parmiter

Abode/Spike Powell 14-5/Ian Parry 1, 16, 18 top, 88-9/Trevor Richards; Crown
Wallcoverings 113 & 115; Lars Hallen 56-7, 58, 61; Harlequin Fabrics & Wallcoverings
(Hullabaloo) 104; Robert Harding Syndication/IPC Magazines 4, 17 top right, 18 below,
19, 20, 33 top, 34, 36, 78, 80, 125; Ikea 102-3 & 107; Interior Archive/Christopher Simon
Sykes 105/Fritz Von Der Schulenburg, 30-1, 35right, (Christophe Gollut) 37;
International Interiors/Paul Ryan, Rex Jackson-Coombes 8-9, 33 below/Tiozzo 32/
Scortecci 62/John Fell-Clark 74-5/Katherine Fortescue 93; David Parmiter 17 below
right, 90, 91, 106, 120; David Phelps 59, 60 left, 72-3, 76, 77, 92 top, 99; Ianthe Ruthven
35 left (Nicola Wingate-Saul), 49, 55 (Alfred Cochraine), 64, 79 (Adrian Csaky), 92
below; Elizabeth Whiting & Associates 60 right/Di Lewis 101/Michael Dunne 108/
Andreas von Einseidel 116-7/Rodney Hyatt 119/EWA (SIP,I Snitt) 2, 28.

All additional photography by Mark Gatehouse.

Index